Keeping Spiritual Balance
As We Grow Older

Also by Molly Srode

Creating a Spiritual Retirement:
A Guide to the Unseen Possibilities in Our Lives

Keeping Spiritual Balance
As We Grow Older

More than

65

Creative Ways
to Use Purpose, Prayer,
and the Power of Spirit
to Build a Meaningful Retirement

Molly Srode
& Bernie Srode

Walking Together, Finding the Way
SKYLIGHT PATHS® Publishing
Woodstock, Vermont

Keeping Spiritual Balance As We Grow Older:
More Than 65 Creative Ways to Use Purpose, Prayer, and the Power of Spirit to Build
a Meaningful Retirement

2005 First Printing
© 2005 by Molly Srode and Bernard Srode

Library of Congress Cataloging-in-Publication Data
Srode, Molly, 1937–
Keeping spiritual balance as we grow older : more than 65 creative ways to use purpose, prayer, and the power of spirit to build a meaningful retirement / Molly and Bernie Srode.
p. cm.
ISBN 1-59473-042-3 (pbk.)
1. Retirees—Religious life. 2. Retirement-Religious aspects—Christianity. I. Srode, Bernie. II. Title.
BV4596.R47S67 2004
204'.4'0846—dc22

2004017287

10 9 8 7 6 5 4 3 2 1

Manufactured in Canada
Cover design: Sara Dismukes

SkyLight Paths Publishing is creating a place where people of different spiritual traditions come together for challenge and inspiration, a place where we can help each other understand the mystery that lies at the heart of our existence.

SkyLight Paths sees both believers and seekers as a community that increasingly transcends traditional boundaries of religion and denomination—people wanting to learn from each other, *walking together, finding the way.*

SkyLight Paths, "Walking Together, Finding the Way" and colophon are trademarks of LongHill Partners, Inc. registered in the U.S. Patent and Trademark Office.

Walking Together, Finding the Way
Published by SkyLight Paths Publishing
A Division of LongHill Partners, Inc.
Sunset Farm Offices, Route 4, P.O. Box 237
Woodstock, VT 05091
Tel: (802) 457-4000   Fax: (802) 457-4004
www.skylightpaths.com

In loving memory of our parents
Marcella and Walter Srode, Sr.,
Loretta and Richard Ashbaugh,
and our friend
Henrietta Lyons

CONTENTS

Introduction

We have always been campers. From tent to tow trailer, Bernie and I have seen a lot of the United States in the past twenty-some years. One of the things we enjoy most is the friendly people we meet at the campgrounds where we stay.

One morning as I was walking the dog, I met an elderly man who was also walking his dog. As the dogs went nose to nose, we enjoyed chatting about the weather, the campground, and our pets. I noticed that he became a bit teary as he stated, "I am retired now. I miss my work. If it weren't for this little dog, my life would not mean anything." He then ambled on down the road and entered his $150,000 motor home.

This man and our brief encounter set in motion a resolve to write that book about spirituality that I had been considering for a year or so. Bernie was already deep into writing his own book on spirituality, *When in Doubt Follow the Yellow Brick Road*. Now I knew I had to write mine. The result was *Creating a Spiritual Retirement: A Guide to the Unseen Possibilities in Our Lives* (SkyLight Paths).

As we have observed the impact of these books on the lives of others, and the needs of an aging population, we decided to join forces to give birth to a new book on spirituality that would answer questions prompted by our first two books and give us the opportunity to share new insights into the power of spirituality as we grow older.

The search for meaning began early in life for each of us. At age thirteen, Bernie entered the seminary and, after completing thirteen years of training, he was ordained a Roman Catholic priest in 1965.

At age seventeen I entered the convent and lived for nineteen years as a religious sister and elementary school teacher. Bernie and I worked together for eight years in a parish. We became good friends and eventually fell in love. At this point I left the convent and went to work in another city while Bernie continued to serve the parish and then spent a year as a hospital chaplain. Our relationship survived separation and time. Since priests could not marry, Bernie received a dispensation from the priesthood and we were married in 1976.

Over the years, one of the pillars of our marriage has been the spirituality that we share. This began as we were steeped in the Catholic tradition of our childhood and religious training. After marriage we began studying many different religious traditions. We came to realize that there are common spiritual threads that run through all our religions. The existence of a Supreme Being, the soul or spirit, angels, the struggle between good and evil, the meaning of suffering, finding one's purpose in life, life after death—these are but a few of them.

We have talked to countless people over the years about retirement and aging. We found that many were asking the question, "Is this all there is?" These were people who had the material resources for an enjoyable retirement and comfortable old age, and yet they were looking for something more.

We believe that "something more" is finding the place of spirituality in your life—finding and keeping spiritual balance. This does not necessarily mean that you attend a particular church, syna-gogue, or other place of worship, or embrace a particular religion. It has more to do with connecting with your spiritual self—your soul/spirit and the God who made you.

What do you need to know about spirituality as you age? What part does spirituality play in your daily life as you grow older? Can aging be enhanced by applying spiritual principles to your life? These are some of the questions we address in *Keeping Spiritual Balance As We Grow Older*.

In Part I, "The Ground on Which We Stand," we present basic ideas about spirituality. It is a spirituality that will help you see body and spirit as a whole. It will connect you with your spiritual self and guide you through the challenges of retirement. It will give you tools to deal with the various losses that are an inevitable part of aging. It will help you see your life as a continuous existence that does not begin with birth or end with death.

Part II, "Spirituality—Day By Day," offers practical examples of how spirituality can make a difference in your day-to-day life and teaches you how to access and utilize the power of your spirituality to attain both your material and spiritual goals.

You will notice that each chapter includes affirmations. We believe that thoughts and words are powerful tools in the spiritual life. An affirmation is a positive thought, worded in a way that is appropriate to the situation. It is repeated thoughtfully during the day, to help change thought patterns and, eventually, behavior.

The affirmations are an expression of some of the main themes of the chapter. They are merely suggestions to get you started in formulating your own affirmations. The more personal the affirmation, the more effective it will be in helping you deal with your life. When I am formulating an affirmation, I sometimes reword it a number of times in my mind or on paper until it says exactly what I want it to say.

Writing the affirmation down can be a valuable way of making it work more effectively for you. A written affirmation that is mounted on your mirror or placed in a book you are reading is a great reminder to use it.

Emphasis in this book is on a spirituality that reaches across and beyond religious traditions and offers practical suggestions for enhancing spirituality in day-to-day life for everyone.

We hope that you enjoy the suggestions presented here and find them helpful. If you have any comments or questions, please feel free to e-mail us at bjsrode@aol.com or write us in care of the publisher at SkyLight Paths.

Part I

The
Ground
on
Which
We
Stand

1
Citizen of Two Worlds

The first step in keeping your spiritual balance is to recognize at this moment, as you read this page, that you are a citizen of two worlds. Your physical body entitles you to citizenship in the material world. This is a world with which you are very familiar. Most of us are experts at navigating this world.

Your second citizenship may come as a surprise to you. Because you have a soul/spirit, you are also a citizen of the spiritual world. Some people think that when the physical body dies their existence ceases. Others have always had a sense that there is more to our existence than the physical body. Many have spoken of this "more" as a type of spiritual element to life. I like to refer to it as a spiritual body.

Your physical and spiritual bodies have been knit together since your birth. When you discover that your present existence involves a dual citizenship, with rights and responsibilities in both worlds, then you are on your way to finding and keeping the balance that is so important not only to your growth as a person, but ultimately to your peace and happiness in this lifetime.

Let's start by taking a look at your citizenship in the material world. Your birthright to this citizenship comes from the gift of your physical body. What an incredible gift of the Creator it is! Biology 101 taught us to marvel at its intricate construction. We get up every morning and take for granted this astonishing creation we call the physical body. As we go through the day, we expect things to run smoothly and are surprised if pain or fatigue suggest that things are not going the way they should.

Along with the body, you have a built-in instinct for physical survival, which we call the ego. Thank God for the ego. Without it there would be few if any people on this earth today. The ego, along with the instruction of adults, teaches you the skills you need to survive. You began with the basic survival skills, such as eating, walking, talking, reproducing, and then advance to the finer nuances of survival, such as gaining recognition, acquiring material possessions, and enjoying pleasurable experiences. It is the function of the ego to develop these skills and it pursues them relentlessly. The ego is good at what it does but its vision is limited, and, left alone and unchecked, the ego can get carried away.

In contemporary society, almost every family has a car—at least one. It is the way in which we get to work, school, the grocery store, and appointments. It is our means of reaching places of recreation and vacation. In today's world it is pretty difficult to get along without a car. It may be a Ford or it may be a Lexus, but as long as it has four wheels and moves, it gets the job done.

Your material body, accompanied by the ego, is like the vehicle for your soul/spirit here on earth. Obviously, your spiritual body could not interact with a material universe unless it had a material counterpart. Like cars, bodies come in all sizes, shapes, and conditions. As long as they keep running, they get the job done.

Your spiritual body is who you really are. Within your spiritual body resides all that is essential to your very being—your thoughts and memories, hopes and plans, and all the characteristics of your personality. After your physical body wears out, or is too damaged to go on in the material world any longer, all that you are continues to exist in your spiritual body.

We don't like to think about the demise of our physical bodies, and some people spend much time and money trying to delay the inevitable, but the truth is that even the most robust physical bodies are only temporary. We tend to think of ourselves as our physical bodies, but part of keeping our balance is to recognize that our true identity really lies in our spiritual body, which will be with us forever. Our physical body is the temporary housing for our spirit, and at some point it will no longer be needed.

When I was young, I used to think of my soul or spirit as a treasure chest that I carried with me. In religious instruction I was taught to periodically check on this spiritual treasure and evaluate its condition. I knew that if I did good things, my soul grew in God's grace and became more beautiful. If I engaged in lying, disobedience, meanness, and other types of negative behavior, I lost some of God's grace and needed to change my ways.

My soul always seemed like something I carried with me but was not really part of me. What a difference when I came to understand that my soul or spirit *was* me! My soul was not a treasure chest that I carried with me, but a spiritual body that was integral to my very existence.

One thing aging does for us is to give us a sense of the passing of time. I see some of the first-grade students I taught now sending their children to college, and I have a greater sense of the progression of life.

Not only the passing of time but the aging of my physical body alerts me to the temporal nature of all material things. I find myself asking, "Did God make me only to age and wrinkle and finally die?" When I reflect upon this question, I come to know

Affirmations

I am a spiritual being with a physical body that is temporary and a spiritual body that will live forever.

My spiritual body is who I really am.

I will pass through the door of death with my eyes wide open and all my faculties intact.

with a deep certainty that, while my physical body will age and die, all I truly am resides in my spiritual body. I can say, "I am a spiritual being, with a physical body that is temporary and a spiritual body that will live forever." These words give comfort to my aging body and make my spirit dance.

Our Spiritual Bill of Rights

Bernie's Take

Being a citizen of two worlds implies that we would naturally have rights and responsibilities in each world. All of us are familiar with the Bill of Rights that we have in the physical world. But none of us have ever seen a bill of rights spelling out our rights in the spiritual world. The following is a spiritual bill of rights I discovered by studying and putting together a few of the basic teachings of the master teacher Jesus. Others were based on the universal law that like begets like. And each one was predicated either on the fact of our free will or on the purpose of an intimate relationship.

The Bill of Rights for the Soul/Spirit

1. *The right to have a personal relationship with one's Creator.*
   Remember how Jesus told us that when we pray or talk to God, we are to go to our private room, close the door and pray to our Father (Matthew 6:6).

2. *The right to know that this relationship with one's Creator is never broken no matter how far one strays.*
   Just recall the story of the prodigal son (Luke 15:11–32).

3. *The right to know that one's soul, like its Creator, is neither exclusively masculine nor feminine but rather is a wonderful balance of both qualities or energies.*

This right is a natural consequence of the universal law that states that like begets like. Just as we humans can only produce human bodies, so our Divine Creator can only create souls or spirits that are like the Divine Spirit.

4. *The right to know that each soul will live forever.*
   This right is also a result of the universal law that like begets like. Since our Divine Creator will live forever, so we will likewise live forever.

5. *The right to make decisions that will benefit oneself and others.*
   This is a necessary part of each soul's free will.

6. *The right to have an intimate relationship with another that leads to personal spiritual growth for oneself and one's partner.*
   The primary purpose of any intimate relationship is to allow one's partner the freedom to be himself or herself, and to help each other grow spiritually. An intimate relationship was never intended to be used to change or make one's partner a replica of one's own idea of how that person should be, think, or act. After all, God accepts us as we are. Why can't we accept others as they are?

7. *The right of each soul to be its own unique channel of divine love to others.*
   Jesus certainly stressed that our Divine Creator has made each one of us unique. Therefore, each soul must express this divine love in its own unique way.

8. *The right to live by one's own beliefs, as long as they benefit one-self and others.*

   In Mark 9:38–40 Jesus tells John not to worry about someone who is not "one of them," but who is still looking out for the well-being of themselves and others.

9. *The right to experience the Infinite by always being open to new ideas and insights rather than allowing prejudices and preconceptions to cloud our vision.*

   In Matthew 20:1–16 Jesus tells the parable of the laborers in the vineyard all getting the same pay. Surely his message is that God's ways are not human ways. Therefore, we should always be open to new ideas and never dismiss them with prejudgments or preconceptions.

10. *The right to know that each soul is a powerful spiritual being that desires experiences for personal growth and is free to pursue the means to that goal.*

    In John 14:12 Jesus tells us that we will be able to accomplish even greater things than he has. This certainly presumes that each soul is a powerful spiritual being that desires experiences on this earth for personal spiritual growth.

What would happen if each of us decided to accept this bill of rights and then live by it?

2
The Spiritual Body

Your spiritual body comes to this earth clothed in human form. Like your physical body, it is the creation of a loving and generous God—it is truly a spark from the Divine Fire and establishes the presence of the living God within you. Like children who bear a resemblance to their parents, you, in your spiritual aspect, bear resemblance to your Divine Parent. Like children who carry the genes of both parents, you carry "spiritual genes" from your Divine Parent.

Within those spiritual genes are all the spiritual skills necessary to accomplish the goals of your journey here on earth. It is here that you find the wisdom to make decisions, love and compassion to reach out to others, creativity to develop works of art and reflect beauty in your life, and a sense of humor to help you see the lighter side of life. It is the source of your desire to be honest, strong, faithful, loving, and grateful. It is the basis of all the good qualities in your life.

Just as the ego drives you to survival

and all its needs, your spirit leads you to act with goodness. The ideal is to always have your spiritual self in the driver's seat. It has been my experience that when my spiritual self is guiding my decisions, my life has a sense of purpose and I know that I am moving in the right direction. Yet the ego, like a driver with a learner's permit, continually wants to exert control.

I have experienced this frequently in my own life. While I have this wonderful combination of body and spirit, control of my life and actions seems to waver between spirit and ego. This is where the struggle comes in. This struggle is actually the stuff out of which great literature and great people are made.

Is it possible that our spiritual body existed before it came to this earth? This is a question many people are asking today. I think that it is conceivable that each of us may have existed as a spiritual being before we were born. I don't remember this existence, but it is likely that I was not meant to remember anything before my birth so I could focus solely on my journey here at this time.

As a physical being, it is important for us to visualize what this spiritual body looks like and how it operates. I see my spiritual body as having a shape similar to that of my physical body but extending out a bit beyond the physical body. It is made of light, and at the center of this body the light is more intense. This spiritual body does not stand apart from me, but it is knit into every cell of my body. It is my spirit that keeps the physical body alive. I know that at some point, my material body will become either too old or too damaged to continue life on this earth and I will leave that body and exist solely in my spiritual body. Death is no more than putting aside the physical body, just as one would put aside a winter coat that is no longer needed.

When I think of who I am, it is important to think of myself as a spiritual being having a human experience. It is important to identify with my spiritual self rather than my physical body. One way to help me identify with my spiritual self is to begin "seeing" my own spiritual body and the spiritual body of others.

Seeing a spiritual body is a bit more difficult than looking at our physical body—but it is not impossible. By the end of this chapter, you too will understand how to do this. We have to realize that our ability to see the spiritual body of ourselves and others depends on our recognition of soul/spirit characteristics. The characteristics of our spiritual body are all that we might expect to inherit from a Divine Parent—compassion, love, generosity, kindness, creativity, a sense of humor, faithfulness, honesty, gratitude, wisdom, and all other qualities that reflect goodness. When we see any of these qualities in ourselves or others, we are viewing the spiritual body. These are actually the windows through which we can "see spirit." Who among us has not been moved by the authentic expression of any of these qualities—from the honesty of the child who confesses to breaking an object to the loving care a father gives his children.

This concept challenges us to look upon each person in a different way. It invites us to see each one's beautiful spirit shining beyond the confines of the physical body. Sometimes I like to just sit back and observe the spirit of others in action. I see so many good actions that might otherwise go unnoticed.

This idea has also helped me to connect with my spiritual self. When I am kind or generous or loving, I can actually "see" my spiritual body. The very act of kindness or generosity is a concrete example of my unseen but no less real spiritual self. This is the self I want to identify with. This self, with the Divine as its center, is truly me. I am surprised to find that no matter what the circumstances in life, I am at peace if I am acting from my spiritual self.

Most of us have lived long enough to look back on our lives and identify people who radiated goodness. As we reflect upon them, we are able to "see" their spiritual body. Look back on your own life. Your memory could be of yesterday or many years ago. Try to identify those qualities of spirit in yourself that make your spiritual body visible.

Affirmations

I see my spiritual body radiating light and love.

I see my physical body pierced through with the light of my spirit.

My spiritual body and my physical body work together for good.

14

Divine DNA

Bernie's Take

Have you ever wanted to put into words what it is like having the genes or spiritual DNA of your Divine Parent? I have. It has only been in the past several years that I have been able to do so. I have learned that because of our divine genes, each one of us has been endowed with four outstanding capabilities. The first is that each soul is made in the image and likeness of the Divine Spirit, which is based on the universal law that like begets like. This means, then, that within one's spirit are the qualities and characteristics of one's Creator. To look at it another way, just as a cup of water from the ocean is the same as the water in the ocean—there is no difference between the water in the cup and the water in the ocean—so there is no difference between the Divine and one's soul or spirit. What a unique gift.

The second capability our Creator gave each of us is that of being endowed with life and consciousness. Thus, as a soul we are conscious or aware of ourself and of all creation. Since consciousness is a function of our soul mind, as a part of this ability, we are endowed with a portion of God's universal mind. What is so remarkable about this second ability is that we now have the infinite wisdom of our Creator available to us whenever we choose to become attuned to it. Isn't this wonderful?

The third capability given to each of us by our Creator is that we are eternal. This means that our soul will never die nor be destroyed. What is so astonishing about this third ability is that it is not something each of us must earn or deserve. It is given to us with no strings attached. What a priceless gift!

The fourth capability given to each soul is free will. Free will does not give us the license to behave uncontrollably or irrationally with no regard to consequences. Rather, free will enables us to do whatever we choose to do with all the other gifts we have been given. What makes this ability so grand is that we keep our free will whether we are on this earth, in the spirit plane, or in any other place of existence. Think about that. The Divine Spirit wanted each one of us to freely follow the promptings of our own mind and consciousness—free to be and to do what we please to promote our own spiritual development. To help us exercise our free will, our Divine Father/Mother set up universal laws designed not to punish us but to lovingly teach us how to use our free will wisely. Free will is a wonderful gift because it puts us in complete control of our life. We are now fully capable of choosing all that affects us no matter what realm we exist in. Because of our free choices, we can never blame anyone else for not making us the person we wanted to be.

So the next time someone asks you, "What is it like being a divine son or daughter?" ask them how much time they have to listen.

3
The
Red
Flags

How do we know when our spiritual self is in the driver's seat? Are there signs that help us recognize which part of ourselves is driving our being? Can we tell if our ego or our spirit is in control?

I believe there are very clear, readable signs to indicate when the driver's seat has been usurped by the ego. These signs make it easy to understand which part of ourselves is directing our lives. I call these signs the *red flags*.

As I mention some of these flags, you will be able to easily identify them. Chief among these are fear, anger, anxiety, resentment, shame, guilt, frustration, jealousy, sadness, and disappointment. Some people classify these as "negative" emotions. These emotions are not bad; just like pain in the physical body, they are signals that something is wrong. They are indications that the ego is having a strong influence at that moment.

Once you recognize one of the red flags, where do you go from there? If you look for the source of these feelings, you may say they come from outside influences, perhaps an accident, an illness, a criticism, unfair treatment by a superior, an unfaithful spouse, or the state of the world today.

The truth is these emotions do not come from outside influences but from our reaction to them. If we trace any of these emotions to the source, we will see that the emotion is flowing from what we are thinking.

For example, when I think that someone has misjudged my actions and criticized me unfairly, I feel angry. Each time I replay our conversation in my mind, I become angrier. My thoughts are fueling the emotion. My ego is definitely in the driver's seat as my heart beats faster and my stomach starts churning. My wounded ego is planning ways to vindicate myself.

What is the next step? It is important for me to understand two things. The first is that this emotion is flowing from my thoughts. The second is that through the power of my mind and spirit, I can change my thoughts. In so doing, I will put my spirit in the driver's seat. The process is simple but not easy. I have to have a real desire to put my spirit in control and be willing to make a conscious and continuous effort to do so.

Since my mind is always thinking something at any given moment, and since at this moment my mind is preoccupied with angry thoughts, I need to reach into my spirit and find some thoughts that I can use to replace the angry ones.

What thoughts does my spirit have to offer me?

1. Perhaps this person, who has been so critical of me, does so because of hurts she has received. Can I reach out in compassion toward the pain that might be hers? Can I picture her in my mind and surround her with God's love and light? Can I do this each time my wounded ego wants to turn my thoughts back to the critical incident?

2. Perhaps my spirit might offer me another road of thought to tread. If I continue to allow this anger to seethe inside me, I am allowing this person to hurt me twice. This anger is hurting me physically, mentally, and spiritually. Am I going to allow this person to hurt me again by holding onto this anger, or can I put it in God's hands and let it go?

3. Maybe my spirit might suggest that, in view of the bigger picture of my life and all I have to be grateful for, it is a waste of time and energy to engage in this angry emotion.

My spirit, an endless source of creativity, can offer me many solutions to the situation. Once I have chosen the thought process I want to pursue, the next step is to formulate a mantra or saying to which I can turn when angry thoughts about the situation arise.

Examples for the three scenarios given:

1. I let go of the hurt I feel. I extend my circle of love to include [name]. I pray that the light of God will heal our misunderstanding.

2. I let go of this hurt. I claim the peace that is mine. I feel peace in my mind, body, and spirit.

3. My life is blessed in so many ways. These blessings sur-round me each day. I let go of this anger that saps my energy and breathe in peace that reenergizes me.

Once you have chosen words that are right for you and fit the situation, begin repeating these mantras frequently. These mantras become more effective when you add a picture in your mind. Visualize the person who ignited the anger in you. Put a loving light around her. Feel a sense of harmony with her. If this is not helpful, perhaps visualize your own being surrounded with light. Feel peace in all parts of your body.

When you first begin trying to change your thought pattern, you may have a struggle. Angry thoughts will seep in around the corners, and there will be times when you say, "I can't do this!" Don't give up. Remember that your ego is in survival mode and will not give up without a fight. Keep going and you will eventually be successful.

I have been practicing this exercise for a few years now, and it is amazing the difference it has made in my life and thinking. At first it was a slow process; it might take me days to realize I was living with one of the red flags. Now, usually the red flag stands out like a sore thumb immediately, and I recognize what is happening.

If we look back on events in our lives, is there anyone who says:

"I wish I had worried more," "I am sorry I didn't seek revenge," or "I never spent enough time being angry"?

At this time in life it seems that we no longer have time to waste on negative feelings. We no longer want to spend our energy dealing with nonproductive situations. It is time for us to put a swift end to useless emotions and activities. The ideas presented in this chapter can help us make the most of our lives during the time we have left.

Affirmations

Every day I quickly become aware of my negative emotions and I deal with them effectively.

I let go of all past hurts and send peace and love to those who have hurt me.

I send love to those I have deliberately or unknowingly hurt. I ask God to bless them.

Overcoming Emotional Stumbling Blocks

Bernie's Take

This chapter about the red flags reminds me of my own emotions. This is one level I really need to better understand. I have to learn to accept and experience my feelings, and communicate these feelings in a way that others can understand. It is here that at times I get stuck.

Since I live in a society that is terrified of emotions, my male mentality naturally becomes highly suspicious of the feminine aspect of my being—that feeling, intuitive part of me. As a result, my rational side is always trying to ensure my safety in the physical world and greatly fears the seeming loss of control that real emotion brings. Also, my culture prefers the more masculine, rational approach to life and downplays the more feminine, feeling side. Therefore, I learned very early in life to deny, bury, and even repress my feelings deep inside me.

If I am ever going to feel comfortable with my emotions, I have to realize that all these feelings are natural and important. They each serve a meaningful function in my human experience. Rather than rejecting and avoiding them, I need to explore and discover the gift each one has to offer me. For example, to feel real joy, I must be able to embrace sadness. To be open to love, I need to accept my fear of being hurt.

My problem, as I see it, is that I cannot completely separate my mental thoughts from my emotional feelings. Even though my thoughts and feelings are interwoven, they still are very different. What I must learn is that I can consciously choose my thoughts but not my feelings. All I can do about my feelings is to decide how to handle them. I can choose to repress them, act them out, explore, express, or accept them. Once I have made my choice, then I can find the appropriate actions necessary to take care of myself.

When I can finally accept my emotions, I begin to feel them and communicate them in a constructive and appropriate manner. This allows the emotions to move through me easily and naturally, which in turn produces well-being.

So I encourage all of you, but especially you of the masculine gender, to work at understanding your emotions. You just might like the way you feel.

4
The One Who Is

When we reflect upon the existence of God, we have plenty of sources to explore. For centuries, literature, art, music, drama, and religion have attempted to convey understanding and knowledge of a Supreme Being. Despite all this information, the Divine One often seems strange and distant to many of us.

The understanding and experience of a personal God is essential to keeping our spiritual balance. It is only in relationship to a personal God that our life has meaning. Our life and destiny are tied to the life of God.

There is so much in our human life that teaches us about our relationship to the Divine. We see our children born as infants, destined to grow to the fullness of maturity. We know that growth demands struggle and pain, but the joy of accomplishment will overshadow all they may have to endure.

So, too, God births us into existence, destined to be one with the Divine forever. Just as our children grow humanly, we must grow into that oneness one step at a time. Our life here on this earth is part of that journey. Here we learn spiritual lessons just as our children go to school to learn their lessons. Sometimes we pass, sometimes we fail. There is always the opportunity to repeat the lesson, until it is finally learned.

As we look at God's plan for us, we realize that as our Divine Parent, it is the intention of the Holy One to be intimately involved with us forever. This is no casual acquaintance. Just as good parents love and support their children no matter where they are, so, too, the Divine One loves and supports us. We can learn a lot about the love of God for us from observing good parents in action. Where do their love, patience, and devotion come from if not from the Creator? I often find myself saying, "If a human parent can go so far for his child, does God do any less?"

As you read this chapter, some of you may be saying, "I know all this and I believe all this, but I still have trouble envisioning the Supreme Being as a personal God. I still harbor some fear that 'God will get me' if I do not meet divine expectations."

For those of you who think this way, it might be helpful to look at your beliefs about God and try to determine their origin. For years I carried a fear of God that came from my early childhood. Those fears were planted by well-meaning adults who wanted me to be good. When I seriously began examining some of those concepts as an adult, they did not make sense.

"How could God be less loving or caring than the people I saw around me?" "How could a loving God send children, made in the divine image and likeness, to hell?" I was left with many such questions and after asking all of them, I found that my concept of God was in shreds. The one I thought was God was not God at all, but simply my idea of God.

At that point I asked the real God to show me the divine face. What a surprise to see that the face of God held both male and female aspects. My concept of God was drastically altered by the presence of a God who was both Mother and Father to me. Gradually, over time, a new concept of God began to form within me and God became for me not only an idea but an experienced presence.

I don't think this experience of the Divine is given to only a few chosen individuals. I believe that our Divine Parent wants to share the Holy Presence with every created being. How do we move from understanding and knowledge of God to an experience of God—the face-to-face meeting?

I think it must come from within us. Outside influences can help, but in the end we must meet God in the depth of our own beings. I can read a book about someone and know a lot about her. But I do not truly know her until we meet face to face. That chemistry may be pleasant or unpleasant, but it is part of the experience of "knowing."

My first suggestion may sound very simple, but I think it is essential. We need to turn to God with all our hearts and ask, believing that God is eager to grant our request. One thing I have learned about the spiritual world, whether we are dealing with angels, saints, or God, is that we need to ask for what we want. Nothing is forced upon us, but all are eager to share divine gifts with us.

We can help facilitate this experience of God in our lives by being attentive to the Divine Presence as it presents itself to us. Perhaps we need to start looking for God in unexpected places, because God is present everywhere.

As we think about building a strong foundation on which to stand and keep our spiritual balance, we need to turn our attention to the presence of our Divine Parent, which is the cornerstone.

There is no better time in our lives than now to examine our concept of God. Many of us will find that that image changed as we matured. Others will find that they are still carrying an idea of God that originated in childhood.

Ask yourself, as I did, "Does this picture of God really make sense?" Does it make sense to think that God is more focused on law and punishment than love?

Affirmations

I open my heart and mind to the presence of the true God.

God is a loving Mother/Father. I respond as a loving child.

I let go of all false ideas of God in my mind and I embrace the true God in my heart.

Does it make sense to say that God's human children show more compassion than the Divine One? Does it make sense to say that God is only masculine?

As the time approaches when we will meet our Divine Parent face to face, isn't it a good idea to become acquainted now?

God as Spirit

Bernie's Take It was several years after I left the active ministry of the priesthood that I finally began to get a clearer picture of who God really is for me. As I reread the Gospels, I noticed that God was referred to as *Spirit* quite frequently. That word began to appeal to me because it seemed to embody so many features of God.

First of all, this image emphasizes for me the nearness of God. If I am close to God, this means that I have a very special relationship with the Divine. God as Spirit is right here, right now. No longer do I have to look for a god "out there somewhere." Now is the time that I live within the Spirit and the Spirit lives within me. This nearness, then, also means concern. It denotes that God as Spirit is compassionate. God is the one who gave birth to me, who nurtures me, cares for me, and yearns for me. God really does care about me.

Spirit also gives me a balanced idea of who God is because it works with both male and female metaphors. God is like a woman giving birth; like a mother raising her children; like Sophia the wise woman. But God is also like an intimate father. In fact, there are some images that work well with either gender: God as love, as companion, or even as friend. The use of both male and female images certainly makes it clear that God is neither masculine nor feminine but embodies qualities of both.

God as Spirit also puts a completely different emphasis on my understanding of creation and of my human condition.

First, creation looks different. God as Spirit, with its emphasis on connectedness, stresses God's creation as ongoing, always active in every moment of time. Creation is not about what happened "in the beginning," but about what is always happening.

Second, God as Spirit makes my human condition look different. No longer am I concerned with being separated from God to whom I belong. For in my spirit I am always in God whether I know it or not; I belong to God whether I know it or not; and God is present to me whether I experience that presence or not. At times I think that I constantly live my life "East of Eden," outside of paradise. If I see myself separated from God, or blind to the presence of God, that is my problem, not God's problem.

To summarize, then, my imaging God as Spirit adds a whole new dimension in my life. Rather than God being a distant being with whom I might spend eternity, Spirit is right here. Rather than God being the lawgiver and judge whose requirements must be met and whose justice must be satisfied, God is the eternal lover, who yearns to be in a relationship with me. Rather than sin and repentance being the central themes of my life, the central themes become my relationship with God, my relationship with the world, and my relationship with others. My life is about turning toward and entering into a relationship with One who is already in relationship with me. It is realizing that special bond I have with the One who gives me life, who loved me from the beginning and who still loves me, whether I know it or not or whether I believe it or not; and who journeys with me, whether I accept it or not.

This new insight, then, is very exciting for me because it tells me that

God loves me for who I am and not for what I do. Therefore, God loves me with no strings attached. For example, my Creator will never say, "I will love you only if you obey my laws, or only when you become perfect!" My Divine Father/Mother will always love me just for who I am and will never ever abandon me. Think about that. It is only I who choose to think otherwise.

5
A Higher Calling

As citizens of the spirit world, we all have a higher calling. We have not come to this earth just to manufacture goods, clean houses, run restaurants, or prepare tax returns. The work that we do is important to our survival here on earth, but woven into the job is a higher calling.

Is it possible that before we came to this earth we, as intelligent spiritual beings, made some plans for our journey here? There is a whole group of people, including myself, who believe this is so. Perhaps you want to consider the possibility that you, too, had a plan for this life before you came here.

What would it be like to plan a life here on earth? The first decision would be to have a purpose for your coming here. I don't think beings are permitted to haphazardly tour the earth without a good reason. This earth is a school and the classes we choose represent the goals that we have for our personal growth. We need to know how we want to grow and what we want to learn. Seeking the counsel of wise beings is always helpful as we plan our curriculum. We will be warned of the dangers of this type of trip and will be asked to examine our spirit to see if we are truly ready. Perhaps we will look for others to travel with us—others we will meet here on earth and who will be connected to us as spouse, relatives, or friends.

Along with human companions, we will seek out beings who will remain in the spirit world but will be mentors and friends on our human journey. Once all plans have been made and we feel ready, we are taken to the edge of the spiritual world for our departure into the physical world.

As we prepare to depart, the wise ones will remind us that once we enter the physical body, we will not remember our spirit home or companions, but they will always remember us and will be with us in spirit until the day we return.

So we take the plunge and arrive in the body of a small baby, and begin our arduous journey through life. Even in the best of circumstances, we will meet difficulties and challenges. Our classes have begun and our spirit will be tested in the curriculum that we planned before we came here. Cries of "Why me?" will come from our lips because we do not remember that this is the lesson we chose in order to grow and accomplish our spiritual goals.

There is a story about a person who complained to God about the "cross" he had to carry. It was simply too big and too difficult and was not suited to him at all. So the story goes that God told him he could come to the "cross" room and choose any cross he wanted. He came to the room and tried on many different crosses until he found one that suited him. "This one is much better," he said. "It feels more comfortable and fits me just fine." He exited the "cross" room and came into the light. He examined the cross and found that it was the same one he had before.

Whenever I hear this story, I am tempted to think that subconsciously we know that whatever comes our way in life is something that we have had a part in choosing. Deep within us, we know that whatever goals we have planned and whatever situations we have set up in our life to achieve them, we have what we need to succeed.

Within the confines of going to school, making a marriage work, raising a family, pursuing a career, and the many other activities in which we engage, we have all the challenges we need to accomplish not only our material goals but also our spiritual ones. Our human life gives us many opportunities to practice skills of the spirit, such as love, patience, kindness, honesty, and forgiveness.

Even though I do not completely understand my spiritual goals for this lifetime, that does not prevent me from accomplishing them. I know that every experience in my lifetime is an opportunity to grow. If my spirit is in the driver's seat, I will learn from that lesson and move toward spiritual maturity.

These facts have had a profound influence on my life. They have helped me order my priorities and see value in even the meaningless happenings in my life. I have stopped asking "Why me?" when things don't go the way my ego would like. If I struggle for a particular material goal that is not realized, I can let go graciously, knowing that it was not meant to be.

If I am laid up through illness, I can find spiritual growth in that experience. If I suffer the loss of a loved one, or the loss of material possessions, there is a spiritual lesson to be learned from this as well.

As we age, those who can accept these spiritual truths will find the golden years less stressful. Loss of family and friends through death, a declining bank account, and an aging body are some of the challenges we face as we grow older. It is then that we most need spiritual truths that can give meaning to a life that at times seems to be slipping through our fingers. Our spiritual values will help us realize that no time in our life is useless. Nothing of value is really lost. All that is truly valuable will be ours again when we return home.

Affirmations

I have everything I need to meet the challenges I face today.

Good things are always coming to me.

Every day I move closer to my spiritual goals.

Earth School

Bernie's Take

During the course of our education, all of us have been taught a lot of theories. There is the theory of evolution, the theory of relativity, theories of economics and mathematics, just to name a few. Merely possessing this knowledge is useless unless we can apply it to our everyday lives.

In the spirit world, the same thing applies. We can have a lot of theoretical knowledge about what it means, for example, to really care for someone, or what forgiveness is all about. But we don't have any practical knowledge or experience of exactly how this plays out in reality. This is why we agree to come to earth school with an outline of the different lessons we wish to learn through experience for our spiritual growth.

In planning our lessons, there is no need to worry about the type of circumstances we prefer; nor should we be concerned about what profession we choose to express our talents. It doesn't matter in which country we live, the color of our skin, or even which religion we profess to practice. This is not the focus of our attention. Rather, we are to be concerned with ways of improving the simple day-to-day interactions with our fellow travelers. Our main purpose in coming to earth school is not to learn how to "succeed," but how to deal with fairness and compassion in our everyday human encounters. Nor are we to learn how to best express taste and style so that we can "outshine" others. We come here to learn ways of improving the living conditions and the quality of time spent here for all.

Therefore, all the experiences we have chosen in our life have one main goal: to keep our spiritual development continually growing. The very fact that our spiritual hunger has drawn us to explore a particular faith, for example, indicates that this, too, is an aspect of understanding that our soul needed for our growth.

Some years ago I saw a Peanuts cartoon in which Lucy says to Charlie Brown, "I'm thinking of starting some new hobbies, Charlie Brown."

"That's a good idea, Lucy," Charlie replies. "The people who get the most out of life are those who really try to accomplish something."

"Accomplish something!" Lucy exclaims. "I thought I was just supposed to keep busy!"

We must always remember that we are men and women here on a mission with a higher calling. We are not here just to keep busy.

6

Angels among Us

I was wading through the basement yesterday bemoaning the fact that I had not yet packed away the Christmas decorations from months ago. There were the outside lights, the ornaments, and the special angel that topped our tree each Christmas. After the holidays, I took her down, removed her wings fastened with Velcro, and safely tucked her away in the box to await the next holiday season.

As I looked at the treetop angel, I was reminded of an early introduction to angels. There was a large chart in front of our first-grade Bible class with a picture of two children near a cliff. The children, who were chasing a butterfly, did not see the cliff's edge just one step away. Behind the children hovered two large winged beings. The teacher explained that these beings were guardian angels and we all have an angel to watch over us. As I grew older, the teaching about guardian angels went the way of Santa Claus and the Easter bunny, though year after year I never failed to put my angel at the top of the Christmas tree to ensure a happy and safe holiday.

I don't remember exactly when I began to sense that there were spiritual beings influencing my life. My awareness not only of angels but of spirit guides was a gradual discovery. I know these messengers from God have been with me since birth, but it was a long time before I recognized them in my life.

Now I call on them every day and often feel their presence. I do not know exactly how many there are—maybe two angels and three spirit guides—but I sense their presence as a team. My angels and guides help me in many ways that I know, and I am sure many ways that I will not know until I pass through the door of death and meet them. I call on them in many situations in my life. Whether I am having trouble writing a book chapter, or I have misplaced my car keys, they come to my aid. They do not replace God in my life. They are God's gift to me, reminding me of the loving presence of God that is always there for me. They assist me as I journey in this spiritually dangerous and difficult environment called earth.

You might be wondering why I mention two types of spiritual helpers. While most of us are familiar with the term *angel,* we are less familiar with the term *spirit guide. Spirit guide* is another term for what many Catholics call saints. A spirit guide or saint is a being who once lived here on earth and knows the challenges of this journey. Clothed in their spiritual body, they now live in the spirit world and have chosen to help other beings on their earthly journey. They may have developed special talents and skills during their life here on earth that correspond to the needs of the person they help.

An angel is an intelligent spiritual being who has never inhabited a physical body or journeyed here on earth. As higher beings, they have an intellectual understanding of the earth and its processes but do not understand life on earth in the same way as a spirit guide or saint, who has lived here. Angels have an advanced spiritual understanding and can help us in our spiritual journey on earth.

At some time, most of us have turned on the radio to hear the report from a traffic helicopter. Flying high above the city, the reporter can spot areas of trouble and advise drivers on the best way to reach their destination. In much the same manner, my angels and guides can see my life from a different perspective and alert me to trouble spots. They know why I came to this earth, the lessons I wanted to learn, and the goals I set before I came here. If they see me headed in the wrong direction, they can warn me and suggest another way.

How do guides and angels communicate with humans? I can share with you my experience of angel and guide communication, but I believe that there are an infinite number of ways that our spiritual helpers communicate with us. By being attentive to our guides and angels, we can each discover their best way of communicating with us.

One of the ways I communicate is by directing a question to my guides and angels. Perhaps I need to make a decision in my personal life or maybe I am pondering a chapter for my book. In my mind, I ask for help from my guides and angels. The answer occurs in the form of thoughts that come into my mind. They may not arrive immediately, but I know that eventually my spiritual helpers will communicate with me. If I do not get an immediate answer, I go about my daily chores with full confidence that I will soon receive help from them. They have never failed me.

Another way that they communicate with me is through a sense of presence. Did you ever walk into a room that's supposed to be empty and feel that someone was there? Sure enough your instinct was right, as you noticed someone sitting quietly in the corner. I get that same sense of presence with angels and guides. This usually happens when I am not looking for them.

Recently, I had a cancerous growth between my lip and nose that had to be removed. This minor surgery was performed in the doctor's office with only the doctor and nurse present. Needless to say, I was a bit nervous about the procedure, as the doctor numbed the area. Although I did not feel pain, I could feel the pressure of the knife on my skin. For a second I panicked and then I had the sense that my whole spiritual team was there with me. Their presence was so strong that I found myself preoccupied with a sense that the room was filled with other beings. I was aware that the doctor was sewing the stitches in my face, yet I was calm. I left the doctor's office with a fat lip and an increased awareness of my angels and guides.

I share these experiences of guides and angels with you not because I think this experience is unique to me. I have heard many

Affirmations

My angels and guides are always with me. I am never alone.

Angels and guides protect me against all physical and spiritual dangers.

Angels and guides walk with me today and lead me along the right paths.

stories from others who have experienced their guides and angels in similar and different ways. We each have a spiritual team on our side. We can increase our communication with them by acknowledging their presence and asking them for help.

Those of us who have some years behind us have the opportunity to look back over happenings in our lives and perhaps recognize the presence of angels and guides. Look closely at some of the close calls you have had in your life. Perhaps it was an automobile accident that never happened. Maybe it was another type of accident that could have resulted in death or at least a broken bone. I can remember one woman saying she felt hands under her, cushioning her fall. She was left with only a few bruises in a fall that should have resulted in broken bones.

Sometimes aging brings loneliness. Friends and family members have passed on and there are few visits from the younger people. Becoming acquainted with our spiritual helpers can help us overcome those feelings because we are never alone.

We Do Not Walk Alone

Bernie's Take

From a very early age I learned through my own experience the important truth that I am never alone. I still vividly remember that special night when I was six or seven. I woke up, startled to find a special being—my guide or an angel, I am not sure which—sitting on the edge of my bed. Without the least bit of fear, I sat up and began talking to that special being. I cannot recall the conversation, but I do know it lasted five to ten minutes. The happiness I felt afterwards was beyond belief. Without a doubt, I knew my special friend would always be with me. Fear of being made fun of caused me never to tell a soul about this until these last few years.

Then in my first year of theological training in the seminary (I had just three remaining years before I would be ordained), I had another experience of my guide or angel helping me. I was sent on an errand in town and was allowed to use the seminary car. On my way back to the seminary, cruising along at around 45mph on a two-lane road, I suddenly saw a school bus pulling out in front of me on the left. My first reaction was to apply the brakes, but I knew I couldn't stop in time to avoid the crash. Suddenly I heard a voice say loud and clear, "Hit the berm!" I did and avoided the accident. The school bus driver apologized for not seeing me. A bit shaken, I climbed back into the car and instantly knew that the voice had been my angel or my guide, because I was alone in the car—or so I thought.

Then as I grew older I was told that I, as a human being, am the highest form of intelligent life around. This idea seemed to me to be smug and arrogant. I knew from experience that other beings do exist in another dimension that I call the spirit world.

I believe that I have four or five spirit guides and at least one angel, if not more. Throughout my life I have always called upon my guides and angel(s) for advice in my decisions—unimportant and important. They will usually answer me not by voice but by thoughts, ideas, impressions, and feelings. If no response comes immediately, I have learned to look for an answer later at sometime, somewhere, or from someone, when I least expect it. It could be something I read in a book, something someone says to me, or, as has happened once, from the sign on the back of a semi truck that was traveling in front of me. It read: God is Love. If you abide in love, you abide in God and God in you.

I must always remember that even though my guides and angels try to lead me through my daily life and impress me with the best ways to respond to certain situations, they cannot and do not interfere with the lessons or challenges that I have created on earth to learn and grow spiritually.

What a consolation it is to be able to travel through life knowing that I do not walk alone.

7
A Sure Thing

There are more sure things in life than death and taxes. From the time we are very young, we learn about certain things in the material world that never change. From jumping off the top of a slide, to trying a superman stunt from the garage roof, we painfully learn about the law of gravity. This law has no regard for who you are. Whether you are president of the United States or a postal worker on his rounds, if you trip and fall, it hurts just the same.

When we are children, our parents warn us about the dangers of fire, but most children are curious and sooner or later find out for themselves that fire burns. Repeat encounters with fire produce the same result. As the child grows, he learns that where there is fire he can get burned.

As the years pass, the child learns more immutable facts about the material world around him. Water is wet, ice is cold, lemons are bitter. In school he learns how to use unchanging scientific information to his advantage, and as an adult he takes for granted so many conveniences that are built on unchanging material laws.

It is not quite accurate to call gravity a *law,* if we think of law as a human-made decree that people must follow for the good of society. It is more a principle of how things work and is unchangeable. Violating the *law of gravity* does not result in some punishment by an outside source. It carries what we might call an innate *punishment,* better viewed as a consequence of not heeding the law.

Just as there are unchanging material laws in the physical world, there are also unchanging spiritual laws. They are true for everyone, no matter who you are. Some people refer to these as universal laws.

Spiritual laws are much like the law of gravity in terms of consequences. There is no punishment from an outside source—either God or human—it is simply the way things work in the world of spirit. If we disregard a spiritual law, we experience the consequences.

There are many spiritual laws and some, I am sure, we have yet to discover. One that comes to mind is the *law of cause and effect.* You might know it as "What goes around, comes around," or "As you sow, so shall you will reap." We know how to apply this to our own lives in terms of our own actions, but sometimes we see people sowing greed and lies and we do not see them reaping the consequences.

There is a lot of anger right now in our society toward people who have not been honest and have lost the money of others while safeguarding their own. To those angry people I say, "What goes around comes around." We may not see the results of their behavior today or tomorrow, but ultimately they are responsible for their actions and will have to experience the consequences. The law of cause and effect will see that it happens.

This law frees me from the anger that seems justifiable toward those who have hurt me and others. It frees me from the frustration and desire to seek revenge against the seeming unfairness of some situations. Between my careers as teacher and chaplain, I worked for a business. Someone in the business was cheating and most of us knew it. Another coworker came to me livid with anger that this person was "getting away with it." She didn't understand why I was not upset as well. I told her that I believed no one "gets away with anything." We all are responsible for our actions and in the big picture we will have to deal with the consequences. Little did I realize that the law of cause and effect would act so quickly in this case. In three weeks, the employee who was cheating was fired.

This brings me to an important observation. I can hear people saying, "I was fired and I did nothing to deserve it." While the law of cause and effect works from cause to effect, (I cheated and I got fired), it does not work the other way (I got fired therefore I must have cheated). The experiences in our lives may happen for another reason. It is possible that this experience was sent into your life so you could learn a lesson that you planned in your life's curriculum.

There is always the temptation to ask the question, "Why did this happen?" Maybe we will never be able to answer that question.

Perhaps the best question to ask is, "What can I learn from this experience?" "How can it make me a better person?"

I can remember when our dear ninety-two-year-old friend, Henrietta, was in rehab for three weeks. Daily exercises exhausted her and bedsores made her time of rest uncomfortable. She said, "Why do I have to go through this? I never knew people had to go through things like this." After she reflected a few moments, she answered her own question by saying, "Maybe that is the reason—to teach me what some people have to go through." Even at that stage in her life not only was she asking the "Why me" questions, but she was searching for meaning in what was happening to her.

The law of cause and effect also has its brighter side, called the *law of compensation*. The law of compensation states that the good that we do will be returned to us. This does not necessarily mean that if I give someone $10 the same person will give $10 back to me. It is usually not the person to whom you give who gives back, but someone else will give to you out of a personal sense of generosity.

Recently, when I was giving a lecture, a gentleman made the comment, "I used to think of God as within me. I am coming more and more to feel that I am in God." This man may not have realized it, but he expressed the spiritual *law of Divine Oneness*. Everything in the universe is connected to this oneness and, therefore, is in some way a part of God. As children we learned this very simply: "God is everywhere." Even though I knew this, I always felt that there were some spaces that were Godless. Not so, the law of Divine Oneness states.

The purpose of this chapter is not to give a comprehensive description of the spiritual laws but to awaken your curiosity to start learning about these laws and begin observing how they play out in your life. Knowledge of the spiritual laws can be extremely helpful in your life's journey and can save you a lot of grief.

Affirmations

I grow every day in my understanding of the spiritual laws and how they apply to my life.

My eyes are opened to the working of the spiritual laws in the lives of those around me.

The law of cause and effect frees me from any desire for revenge against another person.

Universal Laws

Bernie's Take

We are all aware of the thousands of laws written since our nation was founded. Each year volumes of additional laws are enacted. It is practically impossible for the ordinary person to keep up with all these laws. I suppose that is why we have lawyers.

In the spiritual realm, there are also laws. But very few people know them. Even fewer people attempt to apply them in their lives. When they are mentioned at all, they are seldom seen as having any meaning or importance in everyday life.

What makes these universal laws so different from our ordinary laws? The answer lies in who these laws are intended for. The laws of a city, state, or nation apply only to that particular group of people. Universal laws apply to *every human being* without exception, whether he or she believes it or not. It is a law that is completely impartial and works without the need of judges, courts, trials, and lawyers. These laws continue to operate every minute of every day of our lives.

These laws are unique in that they are created by our loving divine Father/Mother not to punish but rather to show us in a loving way how we are to use our free will. They will produce nothing but good in our lives, if we choose to abide by them.

With this in mind, I would like to look at four of the universal laws and see how they affect spiritual life.

Like Begets Like

This law tells me that good can never flow from bad. Hatred will never bring about love; lies will never bring about truth; nor will violence ever bring about compassion or peace. Every time I think or act as if hatred, lies, or violence will bring about a positive result, I set myself on a collision course with this law. What I must remember about this law is that if I wish to bring about joy, I must be joyous; for love, I must be loving; for peace and harmony, I must make peace and harmony with myself and others.

Likewise, the opposite is true. If I dislike others, others will dislike me. If I am hateful toward others, others will be hateful toward me. How much better would this world be if all of us—as individuals and nations—learned to live by this law.

The Law of Giving and Receiving

This law is very simple. If you want attention and appreciation, learn to give attention and appreciation; if you want material affluence, help others to become materially affluent. The easiest way to get what I want is to help others get what they want. This principle works just as well for individuals, corporations, societies, and nations. If I want to be blessed with all the good things in life, then I must learn to silently bless everyone else with all the good things in life.

The Law of Detachment

This law says that if I wish to acquire anything in the physical universe, I must give up my attachment to it. But it does not mean that I must give up desiring it. What I must really give up is my attachment to the result and to any specific time frame for its fulfillment. Isn't this a challenging law?

The Law of Life's Purpose

This law states that I have come to earth to discover that my real self is a spiritual being that has manifested itself in a physical form. Therefore, I am not a human being who has occasional spiritual experiences. I am a spiritual being who is engaging in human experiences. I have also come to earth to manifest my talents, which are so unique in their expression that there is no one else alive on this planet who has those talents.

The new insight I have gained from these universal laws is that life does not have to be difficult for me to learn my lessons. I no longer have to choose to experience the hard knocks of life. There is a better way to live. By learning the universal laws and how to apply them, I can transform my life before I create the difficult situations that are intended to bring about the exact same change. What an insight!

8

Thoughts Are Things

When I came home crying to my mother because another child had called me names, she would quote the old adage, "Sticks and stones may break my bones, but names will never hurt me." Over the years I have learned that that adage is not true. Our thoughts and words are powerful in ways that we could never imagine.

Edgar Cayce, the renowned psychic, often repeated the line that "Mind is the builder." Within each thought is a seed. It has the potential to grow. If we look at any great works of art, literature, music, architecture, or engineering, they all began with an idea that manifested itself in a material creation.

Just as every kind, generous deed was first a thought in the mind of someone, so, too, every vicious and hateful act was also an idea in the mind of the perpetrator. Ideas don't come to us full blown. They start as a single thought. If this thought is pursued, feelings begin to clothe the thought and give it shape. Soon, ideas based on these thoughts and feelings give birth to action. From the seed grows the tree.

This is not the only reason our thoughts are powerful. Scientists have proven that everything is energy, vibrating at different levels. Material things are heavy and vibrate slowly. Our thoughts are also energy and vibrate faster. It is not necessary to understand how all this works, but it is important to realize that our thoughts, feelings, words, and actions have the power to effect change. They are powerful for both good and evil.

Knowing this has impelled me to keep a closer watch over my thoughts and feelings, which, at first glance, seem to affect only me. Angry thoughts and feelings, expressed or not, do touch, in some way, the one to whom they are directed. This idea has been hard for me to accept because I always considered my thoughts and feelings my own private property. Even though I could not always act as I wished, I had the right to feel and think as I desired. Now I find out that harboring angry, resentful thoughts and feelings toward someone will hurt them.

While this understanding has been disconcerting, it brings good news as well. My thoughts and feelings have tremendous power for good. If I hold loving, kind thoughts for another, I can help make his life better. If I carry positive thoughts in my heart for my future, they will materialize, too.

This is why affirmations work. An affirmation is a positive thought we have consciously chosen, expressed in words. It is repeated either silently or out loud. While driving to a lecture, I have two favorite affirmations. One is, "I will arrive safely and on time." The other is, "I will say those things most helpful to the group."

Affirmations can deal with very practical aspects of our lives or they can express hopes and dreams yet to be realized. It is best when they are expressed as if what is desired were already reality. There was a time in our lives when my husband and I were in debt, even though we both worked full time and he worked most weekends. With a great leap of faith, I carefully crafted an affirmation to deal with our financial situation. "We have more than enough money to take care of our needs, wants, and bills." I said my affirmation faithfully for many years. It took a while, but this affirmation materialized in a way I never could have imagined.

An affirmation needs to be held gently in our heart with the knowledge that this vision, or something better, will eventually come to us. It may seem like a contradiction in terms to speak as if something were already ours, yet not possess it, at this moment. However, in the timeless world of God and spirit, this is possible.

What is the difference between a daydream and an affirmation? Your daydreams have the potential to become a powerful affirmation if you can remember to think as if they were already reality, add vision and feeling to the picture, and hold your dream with open hands. Perhaps you are dreaming of having a vacation cabin in the woods. Your affirmation might be "I own a rustic cabin in the woods where I can go anytime to enjoy nature." See your cabin and smell the woods.

Feel how peaceful it is there. Many times in a daydream we do all of this, then conclude, "I'll never be able to afford something like that." In one sentence, we have canceled the power of our affirmation.

Be wary of making specific affirmations for others, however. Perhaps your daughter is dating a man you really like, so you decide to repeat an affirmation such as "My daughter is engaged to marry the man she is dating now." An affirmation like that, dealing with a specific outcome in the life of another, is not only a waste of time but could be dangerous. This type of affirmation may unconsciously pressure your daughter and make her decision more difficult. It is better to craft the affirmation like this: "My daughter's good is always coming to her. She will find the best partner for her."

You have the power not only to affect your personal life but to make a difference in the world around you. Affirmations dealing with the world situation can make a difference. There is a hymn that makes an excellent affirmation for our world: "Peace is flowing like a river, flowing out from you and me."

By adding visualization, you can make your affirmation more powerful. As you repeat the words, visualize the world as the astronauts might see it from space. See a golden light of peace surrounding the earth. Go back to earth and see the light of peace radiating from the hearts of people and bathing the earth in a golden glow.

While experiencing this affirmation and visualization, try to generate a feeling of peace and love that can be extended to all. Include in your circle of love everyone on earth. Send them love from your heart. What a powerful exercise this is for peace. As you gather the love of God placed in your heart, send it out. According to the law of cause and effect, it will definitely return to you.

Sometimes, as we age, we feel as if power and control were slipping through our fingers. We used to cook or help our daughter clean for her family. We used to work with our son to repair the car or mow the lawn. Because of age and physical limitations, we cannot do these things anymore. We feel useless and unable to assist our adult children and our grandchildren in their busy lives.

Our words and thoughts have the power to assist them in new ways—perhaps in more helpful ways than anything we have previously done. Hold a vision of them with love in your heart. Formulate affirmations to help bring about good in their lives. Surround them with the healing and protective light of God. These are things we can do even if we are bedridden. Even though we have to let go of some of our physical power, our spiritual power is always with us.

Affirmations

I am always aware of the power of my thoughts and words.

I monitor my thoughts carefully, so that in my thoughts and actions I will do no harm.

I use my thoughts and words to spread peace in the world.

Power in Positive Thinking

Bernie's Take

If we are going to keep our spiritual balance as we grow older, it is important to understand the wonderful ability we have to change the outcome or reality of our thoughts either negatively or positively. In a practical way, this can be seen in our concept of sin.

Most of us have grown up believing that a sin is any act of disobedience toward a God who is both separate and punitive. We hope that this external God will forgive us, but, in the meantime, we find ourselves ridden with guilt and anxiety over whether or not we deserve to be forgiven. Surely feeling as though we have sinned and are not deserving of forgiveness is not the best way to find God.

Believing, then, that my thoughts can bring about reality, I can choose this idea instead: I have not sinned against God. I have behaved in a way that has become an obstacle to my spiritual development. Beginning immediately, I will work at removing this obstacle from my life.

Do you see how the concept of being a sinner gives me a self-image of contempt and guilt (negative), while the concept of encountering an obstacle empowers me (positive)?

We have been trained to think in terms of sin and punishment, yet these ideas do nothing but disempower us by stressing that we are weak and wrong. The empowering way is to view our trials as lessons and opportunities to choose differently. Thus we can transcend the notion of being sinners full of guilt, awaiting punishment. A sinner filled with guilt becomes immobilized and remains in passive mode. However, when we view our sinful behavior as an obstacle to our spiritual growth, we can still take responsibility by asking ourselves: What is the lesson for me? What can I do to avoid this the next time?

I am reminded of the parable of the blind man. People assumed that the man's blindness must have been caused by a sin on his part or on the part of someone involved in his life. What Jesus said was surprising. He emphasized that misfortunes in the physical world are not because humans have sinned. The misfortunes are merely obstacles on our path to being united with the Divine within us. He stressed that no sin had been committed.

What I have learned from this parable is that there are obstacles to our spiritual growth. For example, if I have violated any of the commandments—if I have stolen, cheated, or lied, or even physically harmed another—I can view these actions as obstacles to my spiritual growth. I can remind myself that spiritual growth is what I really desire more than anything else. Now I have empowered myself to begin the process of removing those obstacles. See how powerful our thoughts are.

9
The Right to Choose

You have been given so many gifts by your Divine Parent, but among all these gifts the most powerful is your right to choose, or what we call *free will*. Your free will is "command central" in directing your life and making decisions. It stands between your ego and your spirit, gathers information, and is influenced by both areas in your decision making.

This is the gift that is closest to the essence of who you are. This is the gift in which you most closely resemble your Divine Parent because it allows you to be a cocreator with God. *Cocreator* seems like an awesome title for a human being. This title is obvious when you bring a child into the world. You have helped fashion the body into which the soul, created by God, enters.

It is more difficult to see that in every choice you make, you are cocreating with the Divine. You are continuing to complete the plan for yourself that God began at your creation. You are also contributing to the creation of the earth.

During any given day, you make hundreds of choices. Some seem small and insignificant; others are life-altering. All are expressions of this powerful gift that gives you the opportunity to create your life in a certain way. Each choice you make and express through your thoughts, words, and actions shapes your life. These thoughts, words, and actions are so automatic you may not think of them as an opportunity to create your life. If you trace any single one of these back to its beginning, you will see that there was a split second when you first made a choice.

The ideal is to always recognize that split second and have a clear idea of the decision you are making—to always be aware that the consequences of this decision are creating your life. We all want to make decisions that are both in our best interest and in the best interest of others.

To make the best choice in any given situation, you need to know what your spiritual and material goals are for your life and to keep them in focus. This may sound like a lot of work involved in making every choice, but if you set up a pattern of making choices in line with your goals, it soon comes naturally.

For example, a woman who is trying to lose weight needs to make good food choices at every meal and sometimes in between. She knows what her goal is and what she needs to do to achieve it. It only takes a split second to make a decision about the food that is in front of her.

A man believes that "honesty is the best policy" and has always been honest in his business dealings and his personal life. He considers himself an honest person. When the opportunity to make a substantial profit by being dishonest presents itself, this is not an option for him. He is so grounded in his values that his choice has already been made.

Our values and spiritual goals need to be so firmly set in our mind that making choices and respecting them becomes a habit. As we grow older, it is good to reflect upon the values that we hold dear and examine our choices to see if they are bringing us closer to the goals we have set for ourselves. Keeping our spiritual balance means making choices consistent with our spiritual values.

Our ability to make good choices can be weakened by various factors. One of them certainly is our ego-needs that are very strong and can cloud our choices. Our ego does not want us to think about our choice. It urges us to act first and think about it later. It can lead us to make an angry response, which we regret later. It can overwhelm us with discouragement, forcing us to trash a cherished project that is not going well. It can convince us that we are not worthy or gifted enough to accomplish a certain task.

Depletion of our physical and mental resources certainly plays a role in our choices. Many of us have had times in our lives when we were burning the candle at both ends. Perhaps we still are. Fatigue can cloud our ability to make good decisions. Personally, when tired and stressed, I tend to make poor choices, such as opting for fast food instead of eating a healthy meal.

There is the old saying "The devil made me do it." Can evil really influence our decisions? It is apparent as I watch television or read the news today that evil exists. As I observe deeds that are obviously evil, I tend to view them as the absence of something rather than the presence of something. For example, acts of hatred and violence occur when love and compassion are missing. When I envision evil, it appears to me as a negative energy that tries to influence my thoughts, feelings, and decisions. It attempts to flirt with my ego, reinforcing some of the negative feelings that the ego produces. It is important to know that it cannot touch me physically and, unless I allow it to, it cannot influence me spiritually.

If you feel negative energies around you, all you have to do is surround yourself with the light of God by using an affirmation such as "The light of God surrounds me." See and feel this light, and spend a few minutes becoming aware of the Sacred Presence that always surrounds you.

Since this chapter is about choice, we need to recognize that it is possible for us to make wrong or

Affirmations

I accept the responsibility that accompanies my free will.

I always strive to recognize the moment of choice before I make a decision.

I make choices in my life that are good for me and for others.

bad choices. It would not be called free will if we did not have that option. While there are mitigating circumstances in any choice, we need to claim responsibility for all our choices. If we have made choices that are harmful to ourselves or others, we can regain our spiritual balance by acknowledging them and looking for ways to make up for the consequences of those actions.

Making Better Choices

Bernie's Take As we listen to or watch the news every day, we certainly see how far we humans have digressed from the wonderful vision that our Divine Creator had intended for us by giving us this cherished right to choose. Look at how some people have chosen to let their egos reign supreme; others flaunt their achievements over their colleagues. Look how many have chosen to elevate their own selves, regardless of how detrimental it may be for others. Look how some have cheated and broken many of the unwritten divine laws that their souls were given at birth. Finally look how many have chosen to use their talents to triumph technologically on this earth and yet failed miserably as God's children on this planet. Seeing all this has prompted me to ask myself: Is this what the right to free choice is all about?

The answer, of course, is an emphatic *no!* The right to free choice gives us the ability to choose both in the physical world and in the spiritual world those things that will benefit us physically and spiritually. This, in turn, will benefit everyone with whom we come in contact every day of our life.

There are two sources that have helped me considerably in understanding the true nature of our right to choose, especially as spiritual beings. My first insight comes from the book *Love without End: Jesus Speaks ...* by Glenda Green. In Green's book, Jesus emphasizes that as I love, so shall I be. I like this idea because it means that I am free to choose to be concerned first of all with the well-being of myself and then with the well-being of others. The more I make such choices, the more I will become sensitive to my needs and then naturally to the needs of others. If that need is clothes, I will clothe; hunger, I will feed; listening, I will listen; not to judge, I will not judge. Overall, the more I choose to be concerned, the more I am concerned.

Jesus also stresses that what I believe, so shall I become. If I choose to believe that each person on this earth is my brother or sister, then I will begin to act in every way as a real brother and sister to them. In so doing, I am choosing to become more spiritual. Thus my soul is manifesting more of the qualities of the Divine within me. In doing this I am also encouraging others to do the same. So this right to choose is given to each of us not to display our superiority over others but to help ourselves and others display the priceless divine qualities in all of us.

The second big insight into understanding what the right to choose is all about comes from the Paradoxical Commandments, written by Kent M. Keith as a part of his book, *The Silent Revolution: Dynamic Leadership in the Student Council.* These points may sound familiar. They became well-known when Mother Teresa adapted eight of the original ten and posted them on her wall at the orphanage in Calcutta. The following are the original ten:

1. People are illogical, unreasonable, and self-centered. Love them anyway.

2. If you do good, people will accuse you of selfish ulterior motives. Do good anyway.

3. If you are successful, you will win false friends and true enemies. Succeed anyway.

4. The good you do today will be forgotten tomorrow. Do good anyway.

5. Honesty and frankness make you vulnerable. Be honest and frank anyway.

6. The biggest men and women with the biggest ideas can be shot down by the smallest men and women with the smallest minds. Think big anyway.

7. People favor underdogs but follow only top dogs. Fight for a few underdogs anyway.

8. What you spend years building may be destroyed overnight. Build anyway.

9. People really need help but may attack you if you do help them. Help people anyway.

10. Give the world the best you have and you'll get kicked in the teeth. Give the world the best you have anyway.

The next time someone asks you if free choice is worth the bother, ask them what part of free choice they don't understand.

10
The Doorway to Life

As we age, we find ourselves looking in the mirror and wondering who the older man or woman is looking back at us. When did those wrinkles appear and what about that gray hair? This view of oneself can be very disconcerting, especially if we see signs of aging as a failure on our part to stay young.

Maybe it prompts us to think about making some improvements. They say that a little hair coloring always helps someone look younger and now cosmetic surgeons have developed techniques to nip and tuck away the aging process.

If the vision in the mirror does not stimulate you to do something about aging, never fear. Just turn on the TV and soon you will be encouraged, prodded, and even shamed into buying some of the hundreds of products that help cover up the signs of getting older.

Since the dawn of civilization, nature has been trying to give us an important message about our life here on this earth. Humans have a hard time hearing the message that life on this planet was never meant to be permanent. Our earthly home, no matter how beautiful, special, or enjoyable, is only temporary. Our existence here will end, and nature prepares us for that ending.

This preparation is seen in the trees that lose their leaves each fall, the blooms that eventually die, the passing of our pets, the gradual disintegration of everything material. This preparation is also seen in the mirror. Are not the wrinkles and gray hair a reminder that our bodies will not last forever?

Personally, this is a hard lesson for me. Perhaps it is one of the most difficult lessons I have to learn on this planet. I hold onto everything as dear—the rose that bloomed yesterday, my pet that died last year, and my friend Henrietta, who slipped away quietly a few weeks ago. I don't want to be parted from anything or anyone here on earth. I don't like separation, but I must accept it.

It is a practice of our society to deny death. Youth is glorified. Products come out on the market every day to mask the aging process. Even after death, the corpse is cosmetically treated so that people will comment about how good the deceased looks. Even all of this cannot touch us as we work through our sense of grief. Sometimes it seems as if we are trying to plug the hole in the dam, but eventually the water gets through.

Much of our denial is based on how little we know about life after death. The best definition of life after death most of our religions can offer us is eternal peace, unending love, eternal happiness for those who have been "good" and eternal punishment for those who have been "bad."

I have a hard time visualizing eternal peace, unending love (even God's!), and eternal happiness. It seems as if it would be a lot more interesting to just stay here on earth where there is so much to see and do. Another thing concerns me about death. I am not sure what it is going to be like to let go of my body. Will I have to let go of a part of myself?

I felt this way for many years until I began to get some glimpses into the next world. These ideas came from many sources, including people who had near-death experiences, visions of holy men and women, writings of many different religions, people who have channeled information from the other side, and historical accounts from primitive peoples.

I think that we were meant to know more about what our future holds. We need to seek that information wherever it can be found. I would like to share with you some of the information I have found and how it has changed my view of death.

First of all, we have to understand that all we are—our memories, our gifts, our personality, our faults, and our will—reside within the spiritual body. The physical body is simply the covering or clothing. If we can identify our spiritual body as our true essence, then we realize that death is simply a laying aside of clothing we no longer need. This will be harder for some than for others, especially if a person identifies strongly with the physical body.

Sometimes death is physically painful. This frightens people, but those who know indicate that birth into this world is much more painful than our passing from it. The physical pain can be lessened by the sure knowledge that we stand on the threshold of a wonderful new life. Anticipation of seeing God, Jesus, and loved ones on the other side can soften the pain of dying.

Every day on TV, I watch soldiers returning home after their time in service. Tears of joy stream down their faces as loved ones hold them close. The joy that everyone feels is indescribable. This was the moment that they and their loved ones had been dreaming about for months. Many wondered if they would ever see each other again. The soldiers go home with their families to share their stories and celebrate their return.

As we approach the door of death, I believe that familiar faces will come to greet most of us and lead us through to the other side. No one dies alone. We will be surprised that not only are the faces familiar but so are the surroundings. We are truly home.

What about those who are fearful of passing over because of their evil deeds? I believe that the only fear in this passing is what they carry with them. They, too, do not die alone. If no one is there to meet them, God sends a compassionate being to guide them through. They may be carrying a heavy debt to others because of their actions. Some religions call this karma. This debt must be paid in one way or another. It is much more difficult for a debt to be paid in the spirit world, and the debtor may feel a sense of frustration over this. How this will be accomplished is between God and that individual.

It is my personal belief that I will continue to do many of the things I did here. I will continue to grow and have choices about what I want to do, just as I did here on earth. If my new life is anything like this earth, I will find great universities, schools of art and music, centers to research medicine for use here on earth, gardens, and other places of great beauty to visit. In my spiritual body, I will not experience the limitations of illness, age, or infirmity. I will be young and able to do all that I desire.

Affirmations

I accept my aging as a sign of a better life to come.

Before I die, I find and repay debts owed.

My death is a joyful homecoming, uniting me with my loved ones who have passed on.

As you age, you can make the anticipation of your own passing easier by attending to unfinished business in your life. Review your situation to see if you are in debt to anyone because of your actions. Do your best to pay your debts so that you may approach the door of death with little baggage and a light heart.

Fear No More

Bernie's Take

Now that I am a "seasoned" retiree, my thoughts naturally turn to the idea of what my life will eventually be like without my body. Back in my younger days, when I was actively involved as a priest and then as a hospital chaplain, whenever the thought of death crossed my mind, I quickly dismissed it as merely a philosophical idea—nothing I needed to worry about right then.

After retirement, as Molly and I began discussing the possibility of buying a cemetery plot and making our own funeral arrangements, reality struck home. I must now prepare for the day when I will no longer have a body.

It was then that we both decided to learn all we could about the new life we would experience in that wonderful dimension called the spirit world. We attended conferences and seminars on life after death. We read books channeled by souls on the other side describing their new life. We were even privileged to attend a talk given by Dannion Brinkley. This man was pronounced dead twice: once when struck by lightning and the second time when he had a heart attack. Each time the medical profession was able to revive him. What exciting adventures he described for us during his visits to the spirit world. I encourage you to read his book, *Saved by the Light.*

Gradually, our own fear of death began to disappear. What we were learning was unbelievable. Our thoughts would be very powerful. All we would have to do was to think of being somewhere and we would instantaneously be there. If we wished to pursue an interest or hobby that we never had time for on earth, we would have all the time plus all the expert personnel to help us make our dreams come true. If caregiving was our desire, there were plenty of souls there in need of our talents and abilities.

I suppose the one person who showed me how easy it is to go through the doorway of death to life was our dear friend Henrietta. Several years ago, she had a heart attack. It wasn't until six months to a year after her recovery that she told me about her experience. She had just been taken into the emergency vehicle in front of her house. The next thing Henrietta knew was that she was back inside her home looking out the front window with no pain nor difficulty breathing. In her own words: "Like any nosy neighbor, I wanted to see what all the commotion was about. I watched as a tall medic bent down to enter the vehicle. When he didn't come out soon, I began to wonder what the problem was. The next thing I knew I was back in the vehicle experiencing a lot of pain and listening to the sirens as we began to move."

"I didn't tell you sooner," Henrietta added, "because I thought you would think I was making it all up."

I assured her that I knew she was telling the truth, because I was on the front lawn that day watching the medic bend down to enter the vehicle. I also wondered why the squad was taking so long before heading to the hospital. Finally, they pulled away with their sirens blaring. I also remember at the hospital one of the medics telling me that my friend was a lucky lady because her heart had stopped and they had to work very hard to get it going again. After this near-death experience, Henrietta assured me that she would never fear death again. She could not believe how easy it was to leave her body. True to her word, she did not fear death, even on the very day appointed for her to once again pass over to the spirit world.

Can you see why I no longer fear going through that special doorway leading to eternal life? I hope that you too may one day no longer fear that same doorway.

Part II

Spirituality—
Day by Day

11

New Year's Resolutions

There is something irresistible about a blank sheet of paper. Whether it is a notebook, a drawing pad, or a diary, it begs to be drawn or written on.

It is somewhat like that with a new year. The days ahead march in front of us like clean sheets of paper, awaiting our markings on them. Perhaps this is what inspires people to make New Year's resolutions. A new year is a new start, and even if our resolutions from last year were not kept, this is a new chance to begin again.

If a clean sheet of paper is irresistible, a sheet of paper that has the wrong marking on it is quickly discarded. Those of us who have a number of Januarys behind us know that we start out with the best intentions to keep our resolutions, but by the end of the first week many of us have failed and by the end of the month the road in January is littered with unkept resolutions.

Our mistake was not in making the resolutions, but in so quickly discarding them when they did not work. We feel that a broken resolution cannot be mended—at least not this year—and must wait until that new sheet of paper appears again next January.

The truth is that from a spiritual point of view, every minute is a new beginning. Every minute is that new sheet of paper waiting to be marked. There is no before or after. There is just now—just this moment. As we age, we come to realize that many of our minutes, days, and years are behind us. How can we make the most of what we have left?

The good news is that the time we have left can be just as important as the time that has passed. Spiritual growth is not limited by age or infirmity. It can only be limited by our ignorance of how it works or our unwillingness to believe in its power.

At our birth we came with spiritual goals written in the heart of our spiritual body. We may have been unaware of these goals, but as we grew and made life decisions about such things as marriage and career, these spiritual goals unconsciously influenced our decisions.

The material goals that we set for ourselves may or may not have been reached. Hopefully, each of us can look back on our lives and see accomplishments and find contentment with what we have achieved. Our spiritual goals are a lifetime commitment. They do not end with retirement or old age—only with our passing from this earth.

Until we walk through the door of death, we all have unfinished business. Our unfinished business and our spiritual lessons lie at the heart of every task we perform. What are these lessons and how do we find them?

Everything we do is done in the present moment. With even the most mundane tasks, we have the opportunity to focus our physical and spiritual body on the present moment. It is only in the present moment that we meet the Divine One. It is with God in that moment that the task we are performing takes on valuable significance.

We have all experienced this at some time. Whether it was rocking a baby or finishing a woodworking project, we felt at one with the activity and there was a feeling of peace and contentment in it. This can be our experience in all our activities.

I believe this is one of the tasks of aging—to find oneness with the Holy in our lives. It does not have to be through extraordinary deeds and actions. It is found in the smallest of tasks. The only condition is that we live in the present moment, totally focused on the task at hand. Sink into the task, allowing it to absorb you until the Holy Presence envelops you.

There may come a time for all of us when our activities will be severely limited. But there is no time when we cannot practice living in the presence of the Holy and thus grow spiritually. We will always

Affirmations

I focus my total attention on the present moment.

I meet the Holy in every moment of my life.

I claim the opportunity to grow spiritually in every moment of the day.

have the present moment and we will always have the Sacred Presence available to us. I think it is so important for people to know and remember that, even in their last days and hours, they can continue their spiritual work.

Every day is a new day with opportunities to start over. Every hour and every minute hold new possibilities if we understand the power of the present moment.

New Beginnings

Bernie's Take

Many times after making New Year's resolutions or after making life-altering choices, such as changing jobs or careers, having a family, or the decision all of us will have to make sooner or later—retirement—we may tend to feel depressed. Why? Because we all abhor change in our lives. We become so comfortable in the way we have always done things, or with the responsibilities or nonresponsibilities we have always had, that when changes are needed, we feel that we will never be able to do as good a job as we have been doing.

Let me take an example from my own life. I started studying to become a priest immediately after the eighth grade. Thirteen years later, I was ordained and was assigned to an inner city parish in Detroit, Michigan, and then as an assistant pastor of a large parish in Dayton, Ohio. Spending nine years there and one year as a hospital chaplain, I suddenly found myself at an important crossroads in my life. I was drawn to this special nun named Molly, and I felt that she liked me as well. Should I pursue the unknown road that perhaps would lead to marriage or continue down the familiar road doing my work as a priest? After much thought and prayer, I chose to travel the unknown road. To this day I have never regretted my decision. At times the thought crossed my mind that I might never be able to help others as a husband. Was that thought wrong! Now that I am married, I have helped people I never could have reached as a priest. At the daytime jobs that I have had after marriage, people would often come on their lunch breaks just to tell me about their problems, their joys, even their successes. They invariably would end by saying, "Thanks for listening." I also began a home-repair service in the evening, mostly for the older folks who could not afford a plumber or maintenance worker. Many an evening, after repairing a leaky faucet or bringing a "dead" doorbell back to life, I would sit and listen as these older people talked to me because there was usually no one else they could talk to. One younger couple even thanked me for saving their marriage because I was able to stop the water from coming in their basement. As a result, they were able to make the basement into a play area for their children.

I mention all these things not to extol myself but to show you that I have not been afraid to change. Look at all the wonderful experiences I would have missed had I refused to change course in my life. First of all, there is the wonderful love of my wife, Molly; the thrill of being able to help others in their time of need; and the peace of knowing that it is usually in doing the little, unnoticed things in life that we are able to make great strides in our own spiritual growth and help others in their spiritual growth.

The lesson I wish to pass on to you is this: Don't be afraid to make resolutions—be they new or old—and don't be afraid of change. Like me, you too will be surprised at what you will accomplish.

12
What If

How many times do we use these two little words? In my lifetime, I have probably used them thousands of times and they have led me down roads I would have preferred not to go.

When I was younger, my questions revolved around my studies and my social life. What if I don't pass my exams or what if I don't get a date for the prom? Maturity brought new questions, introduced by the same *what if*. What if I can't get a job or what if I never find the right person to marry?

As I get older, I find those questions again taking another turn as I contemplate the many uncertainties of aging. Those of us who have retired are all too familiar with those *what if* questions. They seem to be more urgent and important than ever. What if I become ill and cannot take care of myself? What if I do not have enough money to cover my expenses? What if something happens to my spouse? What if all my relatives and friends die before I do? What if my mind begins to fail me? A whole deluge of fears and worries can be conjured up with those two words.

Our litany of *what ifs* sometimes seem like small dogs nipping at our heels; at other times they feel like wild animals that have landed on our backs and knocked us to the ground. Spending too much time contemplating these questions can leave us feeling depressed and discouraged.

The other morning I woke up with an especially long list of *what ifs* in my head when suddenly it hit me. These two words work equally as well for raising up as for putting down. This realization ushered in a whole new set of *what if* questions.

> What if I woke up each morning with the realization that I was never alone and walked this day surrounded by the love and light of God?

> What if I saw every problem in my life as a challenge and I affirmed that good could come out of every situation?

> What if I were convinced that there was meaning in everything that happened to me, especially those things that were disappointing, sad, or painful?

> What if I remembered that my angels and spirit guides were always here and called on them every day to assist me?

It is just as easy and a lot more comforting to imagine the spiritual help that surrounds us, than it is to imagine the presence of possible problems and threats. Not only is it more comforting, but the spiritual help is a reality, while the worries that prey on our minds often never happen or play out much differently than we expected.

I believe that we can make a significant difference in our personal lives by listening for the words *what if* that so subtly slip into our thoughts and speech. They can be the red flags alerting us to more closely examine our thought patterns for useless worrying.

Sometimes I like to have fun with this concept. I call it the *what if* game. I begin to think of a global *what if* and its consequences. For example, what if everyone in the world were honest with everyone else? In the business world alone, this would have vast implications. No retailer would ask a person to pay more for something than it is worth, and the store owner would gladly replace anything that was defective. No door locks would be needed. There would be no stealing, of course, because it is dishonest to say something is yours if you did not receive it as a gift or pay for it.

What if loving and caring for one's neighbor were a priority in this world? There would be no hunger or poverty. All of us could raise our families in decency and have the necessities of life. It would be heaven on earth.

You and some of your friends might get together sometime and play this game. Let someone suggest a positive *what if* to the group and let each person use his or her imagination to suggest changes to bring about that positive outcome. Not only will you enjoy seeing the results of people's responses, you and they can make a positive impact on the world.

You might say these conjectures are simply fantasy and have no value in the real world. We know, from a spiritual point of view, the impact of our thoughts and words. I believe that whether your *what ifs* are on a personal level or on a global one, they can make a difference. Every great idea or movement began first as a thought in the mind of a human being. Every great idea for good or ill began with *what if*. The words *what if* can be a bullet or a blessing in our lives. It is our choice.

Affirmations

I let go of any negative conjectures for the future.

I open my mind to positive possibilities for our world.

The loving presence of the Holy helps me envision a happy and fulfilling future.

From Power to Empowerment

Bernie's Take

Every day of our life we have a wonderful opportunity to ask ourselves the really big question: "What if?" Let's apply it to a big influence in our life: power.

When I was growing up, I can vividly recall being taught that when God, the church, or the pope told me to do something, I had better not question it—just do it. Otherwise, I risk being put on God's naughty list and possibly barred forever from heaven. Likewise, whenever our president or government said I should do something, I had better do it; or else I could be put in jail. *What if,* now that I am older and more mature, I change my idea of *power,* meaning the ability to control and manipulate others, to *empowerment,* in which power is within me; and I begin to take responsibility for my actions. Surely fewer laws would have to be enacted.

What if each of us decided to live by "empowerment"? How would that play out in our lives? Each one of us would naturally act in a tender, compassionate, and sensitive way in all our dealings with our fellow men and women. Yet, we could still be firm and tenacious. Compare this to the idea of "power over" someone, which involves a need for power that comes from demeaning others or demanding that they bend to one's will.

True empowerment means that we choose to see what is really going on and then act in a tender, compassionate, and sensitive way. We understand, then, that all our experiences in life are purposeful.

Real empowerment means that we have moved beyond blaming others. We recognize that all of us on this planet are still in school. Everyone is learning by experiencing life, even though some people are more consciously involved in the process than others. Once we recognize that all of us are doing our best, given our state of development, we feel a deep sense of relief.

Finally, personal empowerment brings courage and understanding to our lives. We allow ourselves to fully live each moment as it occurs. We no longer live in the future by wishing it were here now, or wondering how we will deal with it when it arrives. There is no longer a need to live by fear. We have given ourselves the freedom of a newborn infant, kicking its legs, flailing its arms, and announcing, "Stand back, world! This is now, and I am really here."

Isn't it great asking ourselves two important words—*What if*—and then watching what exciting results we get?

13
The
Gift

Many of our celebrations are accompanied by gifts. We give gifts for weddings, baby showers, birthdays, anniversaries, and many other occasions. They are usually wrapped in colorful paper with shining ribbon to make them attractive. We have no doubt that something special is inside.

But consider a gift that is not as obvious as the ones we give on special occasions. Initially, it does not appear as a gift at all. It is wrapped in strange paper and is not in any way attractive.

At the center of every crisis, hardship, trauma, illness, or loss in our life, there is a gift. We rarely recognize it when we are in the midst of a difficult experience, and many times we never recognize it at all. It is only recently that I have become acquainted with this concept and have begun looking for these special gifts in my life.

The gift is a spiritual one. It contributes to the growth of our spirit and will be with us forever. It may be a gift of understanding, wisdom, or compassion. It may be a gift of patience, perseverance, or gratitude. It may be a gift of knowledge, as we come to experience and trust the presence of the Holy in our lives.

The gift may come as a strengthening or deepening of a relationship. Going through a difficult time together often creates a special bond between husband and wife, parent and child, or friend to friend.

You can get an idea of what these gifts are by reflecting on some of the difficult times you have had in your own life. It may have been an illness, a disability of some sort, or the loss of possessions or loved ones. These crises or hardships may have happened recently or in the past. Choose a particular happening from your own life and consider the experience thoughtfully. Can you identify anything in that happening that you might consider a blessing? As you reflect upon this experience from a distance now, do you see any particular qualities of spirit that grew stronger because of this crisis?

When I was in my late twenties, I had surgery. As a young person, I had always been strong and healthy. When I woke up the first morning after surgery, I found out what weakness was. I could stand up only with the aid of a nurse. It was a couple of weeks before I began to feel even a bit like my old self, and it was a month before I went back to work.

Several gifts came to me from this experience. I gained an inner understanding of what it was like to be ill and weak. I realized in a new way that being weak was like living in another world—a world that I, as a healthy individual, had never understood before. From that point on, I visited sick people with a new compassion for what they were going through.

At the time, I was teaching school. During my two-month convalescence, I missed my students and gained a new appreciation of the role they played in my life.

Another gift-giving experience happened to me when my mother died. This was the first time I had ever lost anyone close to me. Up until then, I had always felt awkward and hesitant when speaking to someone who had lost a loved one. I didn't know what to say. I felt like a stranger in a world I did not understand. After my mother's death, a whole new world of understanding opened up to me. I could approach others who were suffering loss more easily now that I had coped with death in a personal way. The experience of my mother's death planted a need in me to know more about death and the grief process. I have been studying these subjects and hope in the future to write a book about them.

Gifts often come as a total surprise. Not long ago, Bernie and I made some decisions that resulted in a barrage of criticism from a number of people that we know. In addition to the criticism, an avalanche of anger descended upon us. Every move we made to assuage their feelings only seemed to make things worse. The decisions were made on principle and we would not and could not change them. Bernie seemed to be taking all this in stride, while I was crushed by the anger directed at us. As a people pleaser, I had previously experienced little of this kind of criticism.

I asked Bernie how he could be so calm under the circumstances. He said, "I am thanking them for the gift they have given us."

"Gift?" I said. "You mean the stinging criticism, the ranting over the phone—this is a gift?"

He replied, "How often do you have the opportunity to stand up for what you believe in against strong opposition? How often do you have the chance to include in your circle of love those who are hurting you personally?"

He was right on all counts. It was truly a gift.

Recently, the morning TV show was interviewing four young men who had been rescued from an avalanche while snowmobiling. The description of the incident was incredible and they all should have died. The interviewer asked them about their impressions as they looked back over the experience. Each one began to talk about the gifts of the accident for them. One expressed a greater appreciation for life. Another was grateful for the chance to still express love to the significant people in his life. All found a new joy in just being alive.

These are examples

Affirmations

I recognize the gifts in the hardships that come my way.

In the midst of adversity, I have faith that a gift is there for me.

I am grateful for the gifts present in the difficulties of my life.

from my life and the lives of others. Your gifts will not be the same but will be uniquely yours. I encourage you to look into your own life and examine closely what you have gone through. Try to seek out the gifts that have come to you through your crises and challenges in life. It is good to remember that we do not usually see the gift when we are in the midst of the experience. It is in looking back that the gift comes shining through.

Following God's Plan

Bernie's Take

In my younger days, if someone had told me that any crisis in my life would bring me wonderful gifts, I probably would have smiled and gone on with my daily routine. Now that I am a little older and, hopefully, a little wiser, I no longer just smile at such an idea. I can actually look back at various hardships in my life and see the outstanding gifts they have given me.

One such crisis in my life occurred just six months after I was ordained. I was in Detroit, teaching at the parish high school every day, attending Wayne State University twice a week for a course in counseling, acting as a chaperone for Friday night dances at the high school, and helping out with services at other parishes on the weekends, when one morning I awoke to find that I could not get out of bed without experiencing a lot of pain in my right arm and leg. Once I managed to get on my feet, it took me another forty-five minutes to go from my bedroom on the third floor to the second floor where the tub-shower was located. Then another twenty minutes to get enough courage to lift my legs into the tub. Needless to say, I was soon taken to the emergency room and diagnosed with a disintegrated disk in my back. I would need two weeks of traction twenty-four hours a day. If that didn't work, I would need surgery.

Lying flat on my back for two weeks certainly gave me plenty of time to think. At first I was very discouraged and disappointed. "Just think of all the opportunities I am missing to do God's work," I thought. "Here I am just stuck here in a lot of pain. How is God going to get along without me?" I selfishly reasoned.

After a couple days I gradually began to come back to reality and realize that I was attempting to do God's work according to *my* plan. The wonderful gift God was giving me was this: When I work for God it has to be according to *God's* plan!

Another gift God gave me was the opportunity to experience God's care and concern from someone else. In addition, I felt what it was like to experience life from a patient's point of view.

To make a long story short, traction did work and after two weeks I was able to leave the hospital a little slower but definitely a little wiser and very appreciative of the priceless gifts God had given me.

Now that I am in my "senior years," I'm a believer and eagerly look forward to the precious gifts I will receive in each unexpected crisis in my life. However, just don't take my word for it: Check it out in your own life and see what invaluable gifts you receive in your own moments of crisis.

14
The Fog

It is not unusual during these early spring months to have fog. Cold and warm air meet, leaving a cloud that quickly settles over our area. I look out the window and wonder if my house has been moved from its usual spot to some strange and isolated island. Even the neighbor's house only a few feet away is not visible. I count myself lucky if all I have to do is look out the window that day. Venturing out into the fog presents special challenges.

Driving in fog is an act of faith. The strangest thing is driving straight ahead and watching the road come out of nowhere. All the familiar landmarks are erased from the scene, so I begin guessing whether the building that looms ahead is really my destination.

There are hidden dangers in the fog. The back bumper of the car in front of me can materialize in a second. This prompts me to jam on the brakes, and then my bumper is suddenly in someone else's face.

One thing you know for sure about fog is that it will not last forever. The announcer on TV assures me that the sun will burn through by noon and everything will be fine.

There are times in our lives when we seem to live in a fog. Most of us have experienced those times. The fog is brought into our lives by the illness of a loved one, a serious accident, or perhaps a personal loss. One simply cannot see beyond the present moment. It is as if time stood still and our life were put on hold. We lose touch with our daily routine and may feel confused. We lose all ability to plan beyond the present.

These feelings can leave us disoriented because we are a society of planners. We are always planning and looking forward to something. It may be a college education, a career, a marriage, a new home, or children. Not only do we plan for the life-changing events, but on a daily basis we plan for the activities of tomorrow, next week, and next month.

It seems strange to be at a point in our lives where there is no planning or looking forward, where we can see nothing but the present moment. Bernie and I recently experienced one of those times. We had a lifelong friend, Henrietta, who had just celebrated her ninety-second birthday. With help she was able to live in her own home up to this point, and she hoped to die there. For a number of years she had talked to us openly about death. She welcomed death and was not afraid. When God was ready for her, she was ready to go.

A few months after her birthday, her health began to fail. She did not want to leave her home, but difficulty breathing finally sent her to the hospital.

Since she lived in another city, Bernie and I moved into her home and one of us spent each day with her in the hospital. The fog descended and life was placed on hold for us. The rhythm of our days was marked by daily visits, late suppers, and restless nights as we waited for the telephone to ring. A week in the hospital was followed by three weeks in rehab. She worked hard to gain back strength in her arms and legs so she could return home.

We were planning her return home with the help of home care. I did worry about our ability to care for her adequately at home, but I trusted in God's wisdom and help and pledged myself to do whatever was necessary to bring her home.

As we were just beginning to feel more confident about her return home, the dreaded call came. It was 11:30 p.m. and the rehab center called to say that she was having trouble breathing and she had requested to go back to the hospital. After three days of further illness, the door of death swung open wide for her and she was welcomed with open arms by her Creator and loved ones on the other side.

After her burial, we returned to her home. Many of her friends had gathered there to share lunch and celebrate her life. After the last guest had left, a great peace settled over the house. The peace one feels when there is no more pain. So many questions had been laid to rest. The sun was shining. The fog lifted, as it eventually does for all of us.

As we go through one of these "fogs" in our lives, there is nothing we can do to change the circumstances, but they can be a source of spiritual growth. Perhaps there are lessons that can only be learned through circumstances like these.

I learned that I spent far too much time living in my plans for the future and not enough time living in the present. Feeling totally blinded to my future, I felt a greater awareness of the Divine Presence as I stood in the present moment.

Often, out of that fog, I saw a hand extended and was able to take it and walk with faith down a path unseen. I knew for certain that whatever challenges this situation would bring me, I could meet them. I learned that what was most important in life was to respond to the moment with compassion and love. All else would fall into place, just as the road appears before us in the fog.

Affirmations

In sunny days and foggy days, I trust in God.

Every time of trial has a spiritual lesson. I look for it.

I live in the present moment.

Gifts Emerging from the Fog

Bernie's Take

All my life, fog has always intrigued me. It is a time when I find myself feeling helpless and unable to cope with the situation at hand. I must use all my powers of concentration to stay in the present moment because my life may well depend on it.

Most of us have experienced times in our spiritual lives when fog has suddenly set in. It is a time when we find ourselves helpless and unable to cope with the situation at hand. We again discover that we must use all our spiritual powers of concentration to stay in the present moment. We are being forced to make choices between fear and love, between pain and forgiveness, or between walking with someone on his journey back to his true home, or ignoring him. Our spiritual growth process depends on our choices.

What I am learning is that these spiritual "fogs" are necessary to my spiritual growth and development; therefore, they are necessary components of my curriculum of incarnation. For they show that my life is not a prison, but a schoolroom. Since my life on this earth is a schoolroom, every situation and especially every person who enters my life comes to give me a gift by teaching me a lesson. The more times I practice this belief, the more answers I will discover about the meaning of these "fogs."

The message I learned from our friend Henrietta is that when I agree to walk with someone on her journey, I am merely to be a witness and a support to her as she expresses what she is experiencing. If I pay close attention she will even give me the wonderful gift of a glimpse of what to expect as she comes closer to her real home. My mind goes back to the afternoon of the day in which Henrietta made her passing to the other side. She suddenly turned toward me and asked me to turn off the radio. I asked her what she was hearing. "Beautiful music, really wonderful music that I have been hearing all day. I don't want it to disturb the other patients," she said. When I informed her that no radio was on, she smiled because she now knew where that music was coming from. What an opportunity Henrietta has given Molly and me!

The next time you happen to run into "fog," take time to stay in the present and become aware of the wonderful gifts this "fog" is bringing you.

15
The
Smile

You see them all the time—smiles on the faces of those around you. They come in all sizes and shapes and convey a variety of feelings.

There are smiles so shy that if you blink, you miss them. There are smiles that seem to be painted on a person's face. You wonder about these smiles. If the person changed facial expressions, would his face splinter into many pieces like a china doll shattering on the floor?

We remember some smiles forever. These were smiles that were earned—smiles of teachers, coaches, and parents—when we did something pleasing. Our accomplishments made us feel proud under the glow of those smiles.

Then there were other smiles—ones we didn't earn—ones that were given freely. They reached out, embracing us, and we felt the glow of their presence for a long time. This smile may have come from a teacher, a parent, a friend, or a spouse. For me, the memory of a very special smile came from my Irish grandmother. When she smiled at me, her whole face lit up and her eyes danced. I knew that I was the apple of her eye and she delighted in seeing me. Even though I got my share of scolding for misbehavior, behind her stern look, I could see one eye twinkling and a smile on her lips. I felt loved—childish faults and all. I knew that her love would always be there for me and it was, and still is, even beyond the door of death.

The other day I saw a sign that said, God Is Always Smiling On You. This left me wondering, How could I recognize God's smile, if I have never seen God's face? I thought back to the smiles that brought with them a wholehearted acceptance of who I was. It really wasn't the actual expression on the face as much as the experience of warmth and acceptance that was conveyed.

Is it possible that these things were also true for God? Does God accept me wholeheartedly and unconditionally—just as my grandmother did? Recently, I was giving a presentation to a group of senior citizens and one of them shared with me this thought. "God loves us at least as much as the person who loves us the most."

As the days passed, I tried to imagine the smile of God just over my shoulder. This concept of an unconditional, accepting God did not sit easy with the concept of God that I had had most of my life.

I have talked to many seniors who have a similar image of God. For many of us, it is the stern grandfather image that comes to mind when we think of God. This was the image presented to us in our Sunday schools, religion classes, and by our parents. It was not unusual for a child to get "the strap" with the words, "I'll put the fear of God in you." We were told with a warning tone that God sees all that we do, even our most secret misbehavior.

Many years separate us from those days, but fear dies hard, and it is difficult to let go of those early impressions. We need to access the power of both our mind and our will to change our view of God.

Despite some of the things we read, even in the Scriptures, does it make sense to see God as an angry, vengeful, and jealous being? Is this the same God who has also said in the Scriptures, "Can a mother forget her infant, be without tenderness for the child of her womb? Even should she forget, I will never forget you. See, upon the palms of my hands I have written your name" (Isaiah 49:15–16).

Are we willing to examine our images of God and let go of the ones that do not make sense? Reflecting upon our image of God in the presence of the Holy will help us begin to find the true God in the midst of the icons that have been part of our life. Who knows? In this quiet presence we may find God smiling.

It is easy to see God smiling on me when I am doing good things, but what about when I am short-tempered, angry, or irritable? As I thought about this question, I decided that God's smile must be at least as warm and forgiving as that of my Grandma Keefe. God is simply beyond frowning or being upset by my anger or lack of love. When we make poor decisions and hurt ourselves and others, God is still smiling on us, with a smile of great compassion—like a mother who smiles away a child's hurts.

While I do not see the face of God, I can connect with the divine smile. The more I reflected upon God's smile, the more I began to feel the warmth of that smile in my daily living.

This is our relationship with the Divine. We can close our eyes and pretend that no one is there. We can turn our backs and leave God smiling on the other side of us, or we can turn toward that smile and embrace the warmth and love and forgiveness that is always waiting for us in the arms of God.

Affirmations

God's smile is always with me.

I share the smile of God with others.

I turn toward God and embrace the love that is offered me.

Banish Grimness with a Smile

Bernie's Take

I believe that our life is not meant to be filled with sorrow, gloom, and restraint. Grimness is no prerequisite to sanctity. Rather, our life should manifest the happiness of heaven. It should be an inspiration, one that helps us keep cool under any circumstances, and brings us up smiling from any depth.

With this in mind, then, I wonder if we are turning into a grim society. Our culture views as an oddity the person who is able to smile at herself. I feel that we are forgetting how to smile together, either as a family or as a nation.

A smile is more than an antibiotic for pessimism. It immunizes us against the natural discouragements of life. It offsets disappointments before they occur. It gives value to those bad days after they occur. (Some of our worst disasters become our favorite stories later.) So we have to work together toward bringing a sense of balance back into our lives by remembering to smile more often.

A smile is a necessity; it is a diversion from things that bother us. It is a tonic for worry. It banishes loneliness for us senior citizens. It can even be the most effective bridge we have over the "troubled waters" of our day.

To appreciate a smile's myriad benefits, we must experience it wherever we find ourselves—at home, at the store, even at our place of worship. If we are becoming a grim society by failing to admit our own inadequacies, then we are failing to give our children and others that valuable gift of a smile. They are bound to become as grim as we are. Many funny things happen to each one of us; but who would know unless we began to admit that some of them were ridiculously funny and we were able to smile about it. Let's work on reestablishing a smile as a national trademark. It might do more for us than all the law and order campaigns put together.

Always remember that a happy smile creates happiness in a home, fosters goodwill in business, and is a wonderful sign of friendship in the spirit world.

16
Spring Sonata

It was only a few months ago that I looked out my kitchen window on a gray, cold world. Then one day soon after I noticed that some small green shoots were pushing up through the frozen earth and I knew that spring was inevitable, as it had been every year since I could remember. As the weeks passed, those small green shoots were brave and relentless—withstanding snow, ice, and rain. One sunny day, they bloomed into daffodils lining the whole side of my garden. I knew that spring's sacred journey had begun.

The presence of the daffodils heralded the beginning of a springtime explosion. Gradually, all creation came alive. Trees seemingly dead all winter burst forth with blossoms and green beginnings. All of nature came to a great crescendo, reminding me that nothing ever dies. The sap of life runs deep in all creation.

The coming of each spring after the extended period of cold and darkness is a yearly reminder of spiritual realities. As I contemplate the face of a daffodil, I touch the finger of God, if only for a moment. Humankind has yet to create such color, fabric, and balance in one single flower. As I walk down the street under a canopy of apple blossoms, I am surrounded by the unseen presence of the Holy.

Spring is the time for the return of the hummingbird to the feeder in the garden. Robins splash in the birdbath. The stillness of the winter mornings is now broken by the many songbirds celebrating the return of spring.

All this spring, beauty is a mirror reflecting the Holy. A mirror, unfortunately, is limited in its ability to reflect. A mother and child stand before a mirror. As the child reaches out to touch the reflection in a mirror for the first time, the child is surprised to find that the mirror is hard and cold—not at all like the feel of her mother's face.

The sadness that settles over me as I see the daffodils fade and the apple blossoms blanket the ground, confirms that nature is indeed a mirror. The spiritual lesson in this passing of beauty reminds me that this earth school, as enticing as it may be, is not our permanent home.

Recently, a squirrel was hit by a car in front of our house. It must have died from internal injuries, because on the outside, there were no signs of injury. As I picked it up to bury it, I was amazed at the perfection of its body. Tears welled up as I dug a shallow grave to bury it near the shed. We mourn the passing of the earthly beauty around us, and so we should. Our mourning is part of what it means to be fully human.

As we age, it seems that we mourn more and more, as loss becomes a way of life. Either gradually or suddenly, we realize that our bodies are not what they used to be. Strength, agility, hearing, or sight seem to be slipping away from us. We have given up the work that for so many years defined who we were. Many of our friends and relatives and those closest to us have passed on, and we miss their presence. Like the daffodil, the apple blossoms, and the squirrel, this physical, material part of us fades, too.

When I turn on the television, I am reminded of the frantic drive in our society to stay young. Hair coloring, cosmetic surgery, and wrinkle creams are just a few of the products advertised to hide any sign of aging. If we allow age to catch up with us, the ads imply, we have somehow failed. I have talked to elderly people who are truly depressed over the aging process, and see themselves as lesser people because they no longer possess a youthful body or appearance. These people, who have made significant contributions to our society personally and professionally, are now feeling like second-class citizens because they are getting older.

Is it possible for us to see signs of aging as a natural preparation for the next step in our journey of life? Just as a child's body changes to accommodate the tasks of adulthood, so our bodies begin to deteriorate as we prepare to leave this realm of existence for the next world.

Is it possible to look at the signs of aging as sacred signs that move us along toward a new life? Can we be at peace with the gradual decline of our bodies and see this as a natural part of life?

One way to come to terms with this process is to recall each day that you are a citizen of two worlds. While your body weakens, you can reflect upon your growth of spirit as a result of your earthly journey. You do not have to be a carbon copy of your younger self.

You have reached new levels of spiritual growth because of the life you have lived. You now possess new strengths never dreamed of in your younger years. All you have to do is reflect upon the spiritual mountains you have climbed, the deserts you have crossed, and the rivers you have forded to see how you have grown in spirit.

Our physical body is only meant to be a temporary dwelling for our spiritual self. The passing of all that is material is a constant reminder that this is not our permanent home. When we cross the threshold of death, we will return to our true home, which is comfortable and familiar. We will experience the strength and beauty of our spiritual body that we have nurtured and cared

Affirmations

Springtime immerses me in the beauty of the Creator.

I am open to the spiritual lessons nature has to teach me.

I accept my aging as a natural preparation for the next step in my journey.

for here on earth. We will have the biggest surprise of all when we find in this home all we thought we had lost here on this earth. We will no longer be looking in the mirror but at the reality. We will embrace family and friends. We will play with lost pets. We will observe the squirrels and the daffodils, and in the scent of apple blossoms, we will know we are truly home.

Springtime's Promise

Bernie's Take

Our culture surely puts a great premium on the value of being or appearing to be young. Modern advertising promises eternal youth to anyone using their products. But, in the long run, everyone knows that youth, like life itself, cannot be purchased.

However, in the spirit world we are promised a life that will never grow old; a life filled with joy; a life that gives thanks; a life that continues to grow ever closer to the Divine Creator.

Now the thought of eternal life is depressing for some people, especially when we think of the kind of everyday existence we lead here on earth as going on forever. But we can no more understand what life with God is like, than a two-year-old can enjoy a game of bridge. The master teacher, Jesus, tried to describe this life with God as a marvelous banquet; for parties and banquets have been, and perhaps always will be, the highlight of men and women's lives. Some who are already in the spirit world have channeled through others that it is a "life" of doing all those things we have always wanted to do on earth but never had the time. The most exciting news yet is that when we are living in the spirit world we never have to worry about growing "old."

Springtime, then, should always be a wonderful season for us to experience. For we now know that all the youth and vitality associated with it, and promised by the many advertisers, will absolutely be fulfilled in the spirit world. What wonderful encouraging news!

17

A River Runs through Us

I awoke with a start. Fear gripped my heart and was running through my veins. It was only after my eyes adjusted to the dark and I recognized the familiar shadows of my own bedroom that I realized I was dreaming.

In my dream I was a young girl in a war-torn country. I could not leave my home because of the fighting. As I heard the crack of bullets outside my window, I was even afraid to look outside. I worried about my mother and father who were moving around the house doing chores. For a while I sat on the floor by the wall. I asked myself, "What kind of life is this?"

What was a dream for me is a reality for thousands of people today. They remain captives in their own homes, living in fear and wondering what the next day will bring.

We may not know their names, but we have seen them on television. We have read their stories in the newspapers and magazines. As we watch the violence unfolding in so many places in the world today, we feel helpless to change this scene.

We are not helpless. Each of us has the power to promote peace in the world today. How? We can do this by tapping into our Divine Source as spiritual beings with the spark of divine life and the seed of peace within us.

For some, like Jimmy Carter, Martin Luther King Jr., or Mother Teresa, that seed was nurtured and grew into a mighty tree. For many, the seed has blossomed into a fruitful plant. In others, who display violent behavior, the seed lies dormant but not destroyed.

Millions of people throughout the world are nurturing the seed of peace within themselves. They are people who go about their everyday duties—at their place of work, in their home, and in their community. We do not see them profiled in the media; nonetheless, they are making the world a better place. If we want to understand the bigger picture, we have to see their place in it.

These are the teachers who daily go about their work of molding the future generations. These are the hundreds of service providers who show up at our door to fix the furnace, install carpet, or take care of a plumbing emergency. They are the retirees who volunteer their time at the local school, hospital, or wherever they're needed. They are the elderly who live in retirement centers and spread goodwill each day with their smiles, words of appreciation, and kindness to others. We are these people, members of a mighty army of peace that march on in spite of the violence in the world.

I am convinced that there is more peace than violence in the world. As we hear about wars and read about violence in the news, we should make an effort to balance this media focus on negative events with a vision of the millions of people who continue to make a difference in our world by daily nurturing the seeds of peace within.

What can we do in our own lives to further the cause of peace? We do not start by changing world leaders but by changing ourselves. We begin by giving our own houses a good cleaning. What vestiges of anger, resentment, and hatred lie hidden in the corners of our own hearts? Are we angry with someone in our own family? Are we resentful of someone who will not speak to us? Have we failed to forgive someone who has hurt us? How do we sweep out and let go of these feelings that seem perfectly justified?

Sometimes the words or actions of another person provoke an immediate angry reaction in us. If we respond in an angry way, the interaction escalates. Isn't this what is happening in the world today?

We have the ability to take a step back and refuse to respond with the same emotional intensity that was aimed at us. This takes awareness and a willingness to keep our feelings in check, but it can be done. It takes a strong act of our own will to say, "I will not go there anymore. I will no longer rehearse the wrongs that others have done to me. I will no longer proclaim my 'just' anger to others. I will no longer hold grudges toward those with whom I have had a misunderstanding.

"I will embrace the compassion of God who is the Parent of all.

I will acknowledge that there is much I do not know about those who perpetrate violence, and I will let go of my propensity to judge them. I will examine my own attitude and root out any anger or hatred that I may be harboring."

As we discuss changes in our personal life, you might wonder what this has to do with the world scene. I am reminded of the award-winning movie *A River Runs Through It*. As I watched the characters of the movie joined and defined by that river, it reminded me that all of humankind was connected. A great, mighty river runs through all humankind, and while it contains life and hope for humanity, it has been polluted by violence. That river runs through all of us, and as it passes through, we can add our own gift of love, compassion, and forgiveness. In our own way, through our own lives, we can make a difference.

Let us do what we can to root out any negativity in our own hearts so that the gift we offer may be as loving as possible. Then we can join together and pray in our own faith tradition and in our own way for the coming of peace on earth.

Affirmations

I let go of any negativity in myself that does not lead to peace.

I recognize and emulate the peacemakers I see every day.

I am a peacemaker in my family, my community, and my world.

Think Globally, Act Locally

Bernie's Take The common thread of peace, which Molly so aptly compared to a river running through each of us on the planet earth, is truly the desire of all. The responsibility of making sure that the river doesn't get clogged by debris rests with each person living along that river. The responsibility for ensuring that lasting peace doesn't get sidetracked rests with each of us, no matter where we live on earth.

At times peace seems more like a task to be completed over and over again than an accomplished fact. But we must always remember that humans do not live by political treaties alone: Lasting peace depends on each of us. We must search our own hearts for the roots of world peace. What inner sources of strength and serenity do we possess in facing everyday problems, whether they arise from our family life, the life of our community, or from the wider community of our shrinking planet? What price are we willing to pay to foster peace in this world? Like freedom and justice, peace is indivisible. If we allow it into our hearts and nurture it by prayer and action, it will begin to spread to others in ever-widening circles, changing our own lives in the process.

If asked, we all would reply that we wish to live in peace, and yet our days are filled with violence and its salient effects. We feel unsafe in our cities, so we buy more guns. We feel unsafe in our world, so we build more bombs. We know that peace cannot and will not be secured by such means. Even a more just distribution of a nation's and the world's goods would not eliminate all violence. But perhaps this would be a start on the road to building lasting peace.

War is hideously expensive and wasteful, but the price of peace comes high, too. Each of us has to look not only to our own interests but also to the interests of others. At times, this is very hard to do.

You will know real peace when you see a mother coming down to prepare breakfast who finds that her children have resolved their differences, thus making it a real pleasure for her to make pancakes for the family; when a husband and wife go to their first formal dance in fifteen years and he whispers to her that she is the most beautiful woman there, and she honestly thinks he means it—and he does; when your "senior" neighbors report that your children have offered to run errands for them, yet the children didn't think it extraordinary enough to mention it; when you share a few quiet moments at the close of the day with your partner and realize that, while your lives may be hectic, you are gladly sharing a labor of love together, and you both wouldn't have it any other way; and finally you will know that you have true peace when you see that your newfound friends are able to pray and worship in their own faith tradition, free of any and all threats or bombings.

I would like to close with a prayer for peace I composed. It can be recited by anyone regardless of religious belief.

May you be blessed with good health, so that you may
enjoy the beauty of life. May you be blessed with success, so

that you may have plenty of good things to enjoy and to share. May you be blessed with a wonderful life, so that you may experience real joy and fulfillment. Finally, may you be blessed with a great understanding, so that you may be a source of genuine happiness and peace for yourself and for everyone you meet.

May we all continue to do what is necessary for peace!

18
Feathers and Fur

I always enjoy the wildlife that visit my backyard during the year. They are especially active in the summer, as chipmunks fill their cheeks to bursting with birdseed, squirrels play games of search and find with their treasures, and rabbits chomp on garden lettuce, ever watchful for the dog that may appear at any moment. Even though we live in the suburbs, our yard is like a wildlife circus, with the multitude of furry creatures and birds keeping the feeders busy.

A few years ago we had a robin with only one foot that perched on the edge of the birdbath. I noticed that, where the other foot should have been, there was only a small stump. I watched him hopping around the yard and admired his determination, doing all the "robin things" with only one foot.

It was then that I began to reflect upon the way wild creatures adapt to hardships. There is no whining, complaining, blaming, or procrastinating about their tasks. They go about them as if they had no limitations at all. They just get the job done. Biologists call this instinct. I like to think of it as a divine purpose within them. It is probably a mix of both.

As I watched the creatures in my yard, I began to think about my own life and the way I respond to life's small and not-so-small hardships. I have to admit that I often go down the "Why me?" route and indulge in the complaining-blaming syndrome. Could I deal with limitations and go about the uninvited tasks of my life with the same determination as my wild friends do?

It wasn't long before I had an opportunity to see if this would work for me. Late on the afternoon of July Fourth, Bernie and I were just returning from a three-week trip to Arizona. We were weary from three days on the road and were looking forward to arriving home in Columbus in a couple of hours. Just outside the Ohio border, we blew a tire on our trailer. The blowout also did considerable damage to the holding tank just behind the tire.

We pulled the camper safely into a truck stop and emerged in the sweltering heat to examine the situation. We were immediately greeted by the stench from the holding tank. Changing this tire was not going to be a pleasant job.

For some reason the thought of my wild friends—no complaining, blaming, whining, or procrastinating—inspired me to simply get the job done. I helped Bernie get the spare, loosen the lug nuts, and replace the shredded tire. Although we were delayed in getting home, we were grateful that the damage was not worse.

Last spring I was surprised to see a pair of mallard ducks wad-dling across the front yard. I was even more surprised a week later to find a nest with eggs under a bush between the front door and the garage. That duck weathered many trials to hatch her brood next to the front door. Neither mail carrier nor squeaking garage door could deter her from sitting on those eggs. She left from time to time for short periods, and I wondered if she would come back. Sure enough, when I checked again, she had returned.

A month or so after the duck had started sitting, Bernie and I pulled the camper into the driveway, preparing for a camping trip. That morning I peeked under the bush to check the duck, as I did every day. The duck began hissing at me and I could see why. Many little heads were popping up and down under her wings. Even I, who considered myself a friend, was not welcome.

A wildlife expert told me that ducks often build their nests away from the water to protect their eggs from predators. Within forty-eight hours after the ducklings had hatched, the mother would lead them to their "home" body of water. Sure enough, when we returned from our weekend camping trip, they were gone.

A few days later I walked to the park close by. As I passed a small creek I saw a mother duck with ten little ducklings in tow. Was that our duck? I will never know for sure, but I have a hunch that it was.

As I continue to observe my backyard and frontyard visitors, I become more aware of the spiritual lessons they have to teach me.

This mother duck embodied a true lesson in persistence, patience, and courage.

For the last few years, finches have used the feeder outside our kitchen window to nest in the spring. This has given us a "bird's-eye view" of the whole process from nest building to feeding of the young. However, we never actually saw the birds leave the nest. This year was different. As the birds grew day by day, the nest was getting quite crowded. One day I saw a fledgling perched on the edge of the nest, and I thought he was going to fall. In a heartbeat, he flew away. Not long after, another bird took off. By the end of the day, the nest was empty.

All those birds had known was the confines of that nest, and now a whole new world had opened up to them. As I thought about the spiritual lesson of this observation, I began to wonder if we are not fledglings in this nest of earth and one day, each of us will have our turn to stand on the edge of that nest and fly. What a day that will be when a whole new world opens up for us.

Affirmations

As my body ages, I participate in life as fully as possible.

I do not let age serve as an excuse for whining and complaining.

I look for lessons in courage and perseverance from my furry and feathered friends.

Lessons Learned from a Yorkshire Terrier

Bernie's Take

Reading Molly's chapter about wildlife made me realize how often I take these wonderful creatures for granted. I find it encouraging that despite these seemingly discouraging times, more and more people are finding real companionship and friendship with such admirable creatures as dogs, cats, horses, pigs, and birds. I am not surprised, because every animal has the wonderful qualities of love, honesty, loyalty, and even fun in abundance, and each is eager to share these assets.

However, what I have learned is that they will not share their priceless wisdom and great insights with me unless I am willing and ready to do my homework. So I decided to accept the challenge of my dog, Toby, who became my teacher. To this day I have never regretted it.

Now my dog's salary did not come cheap. He required Molly or me to walk him daily down his favorite Elm-lined street. Every day he would mark each tree as only he could, just in case there happened to be a "doggie chick" on the block. The message he wanted to broadcast was: "Here I am; I'm available. Why don't you come out and look me over sometime!" This is a male thing, which I should understand better than Molly. He likewise demanded three meals daily—one in the morning after his walk, one around 10 a.m., and the third in the afternoon; the time was left to his discretion. He also wanted the opportunity to go out at night whenever nature called. He agreed to inform me of his need by (1) shaking himself in his cage or (2) leaning against his cage while shaking—thus he would shake, rattle, and roll. And if these two techniques didn't work he would resort to (3) gently pushing back his bedding, lowering his head, and then repeatedly slamming his dog tags on the metal floor of his cage. This always got me out of bed, on my feet, standing at attention in two seconds flat. Finally, he wanted to know the daily schedule whenever he would roll and lock those "Bette Davis' eyes" on me. For he wanted to plan his day when he was not teaching as well—by playing with the squirrels, chipmunks, and rabbits in the yard, awaiting the arrival of the mail carrier, or just being able to see the world via car or trailer.

But getting back to my schooling, one of the most useful lessons that my thirteen-pound, twelve-year-old Yorkshire terrier taught me has to do with the saying that "Thoughts are things." Surely, no one ever taught him that; nevertheless, he knew a great deal about it.

I vaguely recall discussing this idea in college, but I quickly dismissed it as merely a philosophical abstraction; therefore, nothing I really needed to worry about.

But Toby, in my "dog-trains-man" educational curriculum 101, emphasized time and time again the reality that thoughts really are things. He taught me this wonderful lesson not only for my own good, but also for my protection, should I encounter other creatures of a menacing stripe.

He quickly made me realize that I was the one responsible for whatever happened in our relationship, and that the responsibility lay not so much in what I said or did, but in what I was thinking. He accomplished this by taking every "thought-thing" that I would send in his direction—

whether good, bad, or indifferent—and sending it back to me through some external action on his part. For example, if I think about feeding him, he wags his tail, jumps on my lap, and licks my face. But if I think about giving him a bath, he puts his ears down, lowers his head, and slinks behind the nearest chair. So this action from me, and swift reaction from him, kept me constantly on the alert. Occasionally, Toby would detect something in the mental attitude of a visitor that he did not like. For he knew what very few of my visitors ever dreamed of, that each of them was constantly broadcasting their thoughts and feelings. So whenever he detected a "wrong" mental attitude in a visitor, he would deal with it accordingly, sitting a few feet from the individual and periodically emitting growls until the visitor left.

Perhaps one of the most important things that my four-legged trainer taught me was this: My mind is always much more on display than my physical body or even the clothes I wear. Therefore, as far as he is concerned, I am a mental nudist. For I am constantly on view for all the animals to observe and evaluate.

But *the* most important lesson I have learned from my animal friend is this: I still need to turn my attention to nature and, in particular, to the animals themselves, despite all of the great technology and research that exists today. For I need to recognize the intelligence inherent in them and in all nature on earth and allow it to teach me what I need to know. I will be forever grateful to Toby for this invaluable lesson.

19
The Banquet

For centuries great spiritual teachers have used the common things of life to teach their lessons. Jesus, a master teacher, often referred to these when he cited the birds of the air, the lilies of the field, and the hen gathering her chicks under her wing. How often he began a statement with "The kingdom of heaven is like" and proceeded to use a scene familiar to all those listening. He wanted to impart to his listeners a spiritual truth cloaked in everyday images.

For those who have ears to hear and eyes to see, I believe God teaches us spiritual lessons wrapped in material clothing. We are surrounded by spiritual teachings hidden just beyond our physical world. With a little imagination and vision, we can uncover them.

The last time Bernie and I visited Texas, my brother-in-law took us to a wonderful buffet for dinner. I had never seen one quite like this before. It was huge and filled with long serving tables that seemed to stretch forever. The first one had a base of chipped ice, and carefully placed on the ice were dishes of every kind of salad imaginable. The next table was steaming with the entrees, vegetables, and potatoes. At the end was a separate stand just dedicated to many types of bread. Of course, a buffet would not be complete without an array of desserts. The next table was filled with pies, cakes, puddings, and various sweets. At the far end was the ever-present soft serve for those who like to create their own frozen desserts. As you can imagine, no one went hungry at this buffet.

As you enter the restaurant, you pay one price. Diners are assigned to a table where a waitress takes drink orders, provides a stack of plates, and then sends the customers to the buffet tables. Anyone who sat at the table would go hungry in the midst of plenty. To be filled, you needed to take a plate and help yourself.

That buffet reminds me of the bounty of spiritual gifts that God spreads before us each day. As children of a Divine Being, we are entitled to what is in our Parent's house. It is ours and yet there is something to be said for being proactive and claiming that birthright. Just as no one is forced to eat at the buffet, so none of us is forced to accept spiritual gifts. What does it mean to approach God's table? How do we pick up that plate and help ourselves?

It has to begin with an awareness of the gifts. Many people are simply unaware of the spiritual dimension of their existence. Once we are aware of the spiritual, it is important to realize that it is personal. The spiritual is not some distant, detached dimension of existence, but an integral part of our being. As we discussed earlier, this personal experience of the spiritual includes a spiritual body, spiritual laws, spiritual helpers such as angels and guides, and a spiritual future that reaches beyond physical death.

Once we have been exposed to and grasped the reality of the spiritual in our lives, we face a choice. We can either accept it, embrace it, and claim it, or we can deny it and walk away from this truth. God has given us the right to choose, and even though the Divine Wisdom sees the importance of the spiritual in our lives, God will never force us to claim it. How many times do wise parents see what is best for their young adult son or daughter but refuse to force them to go down that road?

Once we embrace the truth that we are citizens of two worlds, then we begin acting not only from the physical perspective, but also from the spiritual one. Claiming our spiritual body and becoming familiar with how it works will bring about positive changes in our daily lives.

When everything is going well, I don't think about asking for help from God or my angels and guides. At times in my life, I have asked for God's help—but never as much as I should have or could have. What is it about some of us that we think we have to go it alone and fail to ask for help until the situation has become dire?

It has taken me sixty years to start asking God for help on a daily basis. I have discovered that this is a good thing to do even when there is no crisis in my life. A daily infusion of divine help can often avert a crisis.

The same is true for asking help from my angels and guides. They are my unseen companions. I trust them to lead me in the right direction spiritually, and have my best interest at heart. They have always been on duty in my life, but there is so much more that they can and will do if asked. It has taken me a long time to learn this, but they would tell you that I am making up for lost time now.

Finally, after we have recognized the spiritual gifts, claimed them, and asked for help, it is appropriate for us to express thanks to God and to our angels and guides. Our appreciation for all that we have will be enhanced by a simple prayer of gratitude in the morning and at night.

Affirmations

I open my mind and my heart to the presence of the spiritual gifts around me.

I claim the spiritual gifts available to me.

I am grateful to God for the many material and spiritual blessings in my life.

Spiritual Celebrations

Bernie's Take

Everybody loves a party. Just imagine the tailgate parties before a sporting event, or the giant parties after a political victory. There are birthday, anniversary, and wedding parties, just to name a few. If celebrations play such an important role in our lives here on earth, then celebrations should play just as important a role in our lives in the spirit world.

For some of us, the idea of a party or banquet in the spirit world is new, yet wonderfully welcome; for others, the party idea seems ridiculous. However, for people seeking to keep their spiritual balance, the thought of a party in the hereafter doesn't sound that bad at all.

As Molly mentioned, it is important for all of us to be aware of the spiritual dimension of our existence. And part of that awareness means recognizing outstanding achievements in the spirit world though celebrations. Whether we choose to attend such a celebration is entirely up to us. But I think that we would be a lot happier if we chose to celebrate. This also gives us a different idea of our Creator. No longer can God be thought of as just a somber taskmaster but rather as someone who loves to see all beings happy and content, even in the spirit world.

20

A Room with a View

When I entered the convent, my first teacher in religious life was Sister Cecilia. She was a very wise and compassionate woman, but I know that much of the wisdom she imparted went right over the heads of the wide-eyed seventeen- and eighteen-year-old girls she was teaching. It is only now, in my sixties, that I can truly appreciate her wisdom. I like to recall some of her favorite themes. One she often quoted was this: "Two men looked out from the prison bars, one saw mud and the other saw stars."

Many times we have a chance to look at our lives from two points of view. It is surprising how different the exact same scenario can look from two different perspectives.

The other day I was worried about something. I was in a position where I had to make an important decision, yet I could not see any viable options. It was a worry that preoccupied me to the point where my stomach was churning and I was spending sleepless nights exploring all the possible consequences. I was sitting at the computer trying to write a newsletter but wasn't getting much done, so I decided to take a walk.

During those forty minutes, I made a promise to myself that I would think only of the blessings in my life. As I started down the street, I reflected upon all the special people in my life, starting with my loving and devoted husband, my relatives, my friends, and my professional colleagues who have supported and helped me in endless ways.

I recalled the many students during my teaching career, who taught me as I taught them, challenging me to grow in so many ways. Others in my life who have been a gift to me are the hospital patients and their families who shared special moments with me. These are people who taught me about living and courage in the face of illness and death.

I also began to reflect upon the gifts that have been given to me personally—my talents, skills, health, education, interests, and life itself. I not only have sufficient food, clothing, and shelter, but many conveniences support my life in comfort. What a blessing to go to bed at night feeling safe and to wake up to the joy of living another day.

As I counted my blessings, I found myself looking at the spiritual opportunities that have been available to me during my lifetime—in particular, to know and experience the loving presence of God in this life and the promise of a future life after I pass through the door of death.

By the time I returned from the walk, the situation that I was so worried about seemed small in comparison to all that I had received. I was amazed at how forty minutes of "mind control" (forcing myself to dwell on the blessings in my life) had made such a difference. My perspective shifted and I could see my life from a new point of view. My heart felt lighter and my confidence was higher. I had coped with difficult situations in my life before, and I would cope with this one as well.

Not only did I reflect upon the blessings in my life, but I also held a sense of gratitude to God in my heart. I had never before taken time to focus for any length of time on these thoughts. Since gratitude is a quality of the spiritual body, during my walk when I was engaged in gratitude, I was consciously living from my spiritual center.

This gave me an insight into the power of my spiritual body. What would happen if I made an effort to consciously live by expressing those qualities of the spiritual body? What if I consciously lived compassion, honesty, forgiveness, gratitude, creativity, faithfulness, wisdom, and the other qualities of spirit? Is it possible to "be" these qualities? What would happen if I tried to "be" compassion? Of course, this is possible because compassion is already there in my spirit, waiting to be activated. The more I use it, the more it grows.

Recently, a friend of mine who had turned ninety was asked to what he attributed his longevity. He said, "I wake up every morning with a grateful heart." This is a person who does much good in the community and sends out a spiritually uplifting message to his friends every week over the Internet.

Living from our spiritual center will not change most of the circumstances of our lives. Hard things will still be a part of our lives. When I see difficulties coming, I tend to groan within and without. By contrast, Bernie looks at these hills and valleys in life as challenges, rather than problems, and he has helped me to see them differently.

These challenges offer us the opportunity to learn and grow. We have within our spiritual bodies all that we need to meet each challenge and to progress spiritually. When we try to live from our spiritual center, we are better prepared to address the difficulties of life.

Challenges may get a bit messy at times, and our talents, skills, patience, and faith may be stretched further than we thought possible. Yet with all the mud visible, we will still be able to see the stars.

Affirmations

Today I will live from my spiritual center.

There is always more than one way of looking at my life.

I always have a choice in the way I deal with problems in my life.

Seeing Spirituality in All Humanity

Bernie's Take

Perhaps most of us dream of the day when we are able to look out a window in our room and see the lovely ocean beckoning to us as the tide comes and goes, or watch the brilliant sunrise in the morning or the enchanting sunset in the evening.

On the other hand, some of us may prefer not to have a room with such a view because of all the noise of the roaring water, the brightness of the sunrise as it wakes us up in the morning, or the strangeness in the sky as the sun sets each evening.

Whether we enjoy the view or dislike the view depends on our attitude. A secret, then, in keeping our spiritual balance as we grow older is to watch our attitude. Let's see how this plays out in our everyday lives, especially in regard to children and adults with physical or mental challenges.

Are we willing to forget our troubles long enough to help people with these kinds of challenges? These people are often inadvertently left out of normal activities, which can make them feel rejected because they are different.

I have heard parents of a disabled child say that their child is fine; it is nothing serious. Just get to know the child and see what a lovely little boy or girl he or she is. Oftentimes, people do not understand; they don't seem to know how to act, or how to help. They are simply at a loss as how to speak to or how to be friendly to such a child. They do not realize that these children are more normal than abnormal and long to be treated exactly like other children.

As a hospital chaplain, I had the opportunity to get to know a young girl with developmental disabilities whom I will call Rita. During one of Rita's hospital stays, her mother told me that she noticed that Rita was very happy this particular day.

"Oh Mommy," Rita said, "I have the nicest friend here. You'll meet her this afternoon."

"But Rita," her mother said, "you have many friends here: the doctors and nurses."

"They're nice," Rita said, "but they are not my friends. This lady stops in to visit and talk with me."

So her mother was very eager to meet this new friend who had made her little girl so happy. Suddenly she heard the swishing of a mop and the rattle of a bucket. Then she saw a wide generous smile on a face above a blue and white uniform. "Hi, Rita! How's my girl today?"

Rita responded with a torrent of words, telling her about a TV program that she had liked. It was an effort for her mother to restrain her tears. Later, in the hall, the cleaning lady I will call Jane related how she had little chats with Rita; how she kept an eye on her just in case she might need her. Rita's mother's heart overflowed with gratitude to this woman who loved Rita for who she was. Jane had indeed learned to know and love Rita.

I, also, have made a wonderful friend I will call Jim. He is nearly twenty-five years old and has cerebral palsy but is still able to do his own grocery shopping. I would often see him waiting for a special bus to transport him and his groceries back home. At first I would smile and say, "Hi." He would smile in return. After a few weeks he motioned for me to sit next to him. He asked me my name, and I, his. Then he proceeded to tell me some of the highlights of his week. There was a particular baseball game he was able to see on TV or a favorite game show or movie he liked. One day he was so excited. He couldn't wait to tell me that he was going to New York to see the Yankees play and then see a Broadway show while in the big city. On one occasion for some reason, I didn't see him sitting in his usual spot. Before long I heard someone yelling and waving his hands with a big smile on his face. He just wanted to say, "Hi." I haven't seen him for several months now. I really miss talking to my buddy. I remember to pray for him every day, praying that he continues to be able to bring joy into the lives of everyone he meets.

So you see. It is the kind of attitude we have that enables us to see differently from our room with a view.

21
Sacred Space

In a week, I may walk into many different buildings—a school, a bank, a store, a library, to name a few—but none of them has the same aura about them as a place of worship. Every time I enter a place of worship, I am struck by a sense of the Holy. Sometimes the hushed silence of the place adds a feeling of divine mystery. Many times there is a sense of being in the presence of the Holy.

Now a church, a synagogue, or a mosque is structurally designed to focus one's thoughts on the spiritual and eternal. It may be the placement of the windows, the use of glass or stone, or the addition of flowers or symbols that represent religious concepts.

When I enter this place, it is as if a sacred space opens up around me and I am in another world. Is it the power of all the prayers that have been voiced there, or is it the listening presence of God?

So many times during the day when we want or need to communicate with God, we cannot go to our place of worship.

What I have come to realize is that our house of worship is not the only place that we can have this experience. Whenever and wherever we turn to God in prayer or meditation, a spiritual corridor opens between ourselves and the Holy, creating a sacred space around us.

Where do we begin to find this space? First, we have to believe that it is there. Once we believe in its presence, the next step is to visualize it. What is it like?

As I think of this special place, I am reminded of when we were children. In the summertime we would make a tent by throwing an old sheet or blanket over the clothesline. We anchored it to the ground with clothespins pounded into the edges. Our tent provided us with a special space, sheltered from the rest of the world, where we could play games and tell secrets.

Our prayer space could take on the feeling of a tent in which we cut off the outside world to commune with the Sacred. Wherever we are, with the use of our imagination, we can construct a sacred place around us.

Most likely, each of us will visualize it differently. I see it as a gentle light surrounding me and leaving my vision blocked from my surroundings. It is a place that is peaceful and helps me focus on communication with the Divine. I spent many years wondering if God was listening to me. As I enter this sacred space in prayer now, I have no doubt that God is present, and listening to me.

If a tent is not your style, you can create a place of worship only limited by your imagination. This place can be as simple or elaborate as you wish. One person told me about her place of worship within. She designed a room of marble with high windows that illuminated it. In the center was a low table made of marble with a pillow in front of the table. When she meditated, she saw herself sitting on the pillow. Her structure was free of distraction yet grand in scale.

Others have said their place of worship was in nature. They close their eyes and see themselves at the foot of a mountain or by a waterfall. They may be taking a walk deep in the woods or sitting in the middle of the desert in bloom. As they are surrounded by the beauty of nature, they sense the presence of the Holy.

Some people designate an actual physical place for prayer. They set aside a room or a special chair that they use as their place of worship. Entering that room or sitting in that chair prepares them for prayer. While some begin prayer with folded hands or bowed heads, others may light a candle or burn incense to enhance their prayer experience.

As you consider your private place of prayer or worship, it is important to find what is right for you personally. We may have the space and inclination to create an actual material space where we can connect to the Holy in our lives.

There is an advantage to creating a space within your mind. This place is always with you. As we grow older, we do not know where life may take us. We see many of our friends and relatives in the hospital or nursing homes. The time may come when you may have to leave your special room or chair, you may not be able to visit your local house of worship. It is then that the special place of prayer within you will sustain and comfort you. A place will always be available where you can pray, meditate, and experience God's presence.

Affirmations

I create a special place of worship within that is right for me.

As I pray, a sacred space opens around me.

As I open my mind and heart in prayer, I am surrounded by a holy light.

A Spiritual Retreat All Your Own

Bernie's Take

As part of my seminary training, twice each day our group would assemble in chapel for a special time of communication with God called meditation. On occasion, someone would read excerpts from a spiritual book, pausing from time to time for the thoughts to sink in. Most of the time it was left up to us how we wished to commune with our God.

Sometime during those thirteen years, I began to realize that I didn't need to be in chapel to talk with God. I could converse with my Divine Creator after breakfast while making my bed; in the five minutes I had to get to my next class; while getting ready to go to my assigned job every day—be that work in the kitchen or in the house, on the farm, as part of the paint crew or the general maintenance detail—or even during a quiet walk outside just before evening prayers. The whole atmosphere of seminary life was a sacred place in which it was very easy to turn my thoughts to God.

Having been away from that atmosphere for many, many years now, my favorite sacred place is right within me. It is a place I designed myself. It has lots of green grass, hundreds of flowers of every color and shape, and a babbling brook running freely. Any time I feel stressed or need to "get away," I go to my sacred space. There I can forget all my worries and frustrations and just relax. I know I am perfectly safe, for I am with my Creator, who loves me just the way I am. There is no need for excuses;

there is neither judgment nor blame, just peace and contentment. After staying there for a while, I am ready to come back and face all my challenges with more determination than ever.

I encourage each of you to find a special place that is truly sacred for you. Experience for yourself the peace and contentment that Molly and I are trying to express when such a place is found.

22
Crisis in America

September 11 will never be the same in the minds and hearts of Americans after 2001. On that date we were shaken to our very roots as we watched and learned about the attack on our country. Television, radio, and the newspapers made us aware of the suffering of our brothers and sisters in New York; Washington, D.C.; and all parts of the United States and the world who lost loved ones in the terrorist attacks.

The endless discussions about who, why, and how surrounding these events led to many questions of a spiritual nature. Some of the questions I heard most often were: Did God cause this suffering? How could a loving God permit this to happen? If God is all-powerful, why wasn't this stopped before it happened? Where is God in all this suffering?

I don't presume to know the answers to these questions, but I do believe that there are some truths that can help us explore the mystery of this terrible happening. The questions surrounding 9/11 can be summed up this way: If there is a God and that God is good and all-powerful, why did this happen?

Statistics tell us that most people believe in a Supreme Being, whether that being is called Yahweh, Allah, Higher Power, or God. Of this group, most believe that God is good and all-powerful. Many are puzzled when bad things happen to the people of God's creation.

I do not believe that God plans or causes suffering, just as any good parents would not cause suffering for their children. Nevertheless, good parents would not shield their children from the hard knocks of life necessary for growth.

I often think of parents who send their children off to college. I am sure that many of you can relate to the feelings of anxiety, worry, and concern as your children were on their own for the first time as adults. Suddenly they are thrown into the world of managing their time and money, being responsible for their assignments, and negotiating the perils of social life. You are no longer on the scene to tell them what to do, to supervise their activities. You know that there are going to be some rough times and some failures. Yet are you going to take that college experience away from them?

When God sends us to earth school, it is with all the love and concern that the parent sends a son or daughter to college. God knows that there are going to be some tough times; we may make some bad choices; we may even flunk out this time around. In the midst of all this, God has made us a promise. The promise is that God will always be with us. God's love, guidance, and strength will sustain us no matter where we are led by our decisions or the decisions of others. Just as the parent is still behind the child who has gone off to college, so, too, God is behind us.

We live in an imperfect world—a world that is continually moving toward divine completion. We groan and strain, sometimes moving two steps forward and one step back. When we entered this world, we knew this at an unconscious level and agreed to come with the sacred commission of making it a better place. The suffering we experience is part of the struggle to leave the world a better place than we found it. It is not God causing the suffering, but the pain of birth that we all experience as we bear love into the world.

We could not accomplish this task without the most precious gift of free will given to us by God. The problem, of course, with free will is that there are those who will make bad choices. There are those who choose to go down roads of destruction for themselves and for others, as we have seen in the events of 9/11. Will God interfere with the free will of some? But which ones? Have we not all made poor decisions at times?

Where is God in all this? God was there all along. God was in the hearts and hands of every person who reached out to help another during the 9/11 crisis. God traveled with a group who drove nonstop from Dallas to bring skin grafts to New York. God was going up the stairs of the World Trade Center to rescue others while most were running down the stairs for their lives. God dressed the wounds and comforted the frightened immediately after the blast. God worked fifteen- and twenty-hour days in search and rescue. God was seen in the children who gave buckets of pennies they had been saving for something special, and in the little boy who gave his allowance to the relief effort. There are hundreds of stories of God's presence and love in the midst of these tragic events.

Little did we realize that 9/11 was the beginning of an extended period of crisis in our country. That event, like an earthquake, was followed by the aftershocks of war in Afghanistan and the conflict in Iraq. These devastating experiences have touched every family and every community in some way. The pain of separation and loss has left us all looking at the deeper issues in our lives.

I have heard many talk about the clarity with which they see the most important things in their lives and how trivial were some of yesterday's pursuits. I wake up every morning grateful that I am here and relish the daily routine that used to seem tiring or boring at times. Every "good-bye" to a loved one is said with the awareness that it might be the

Affirmations

God's support is always present in the hard times of my life.

I send light and love today to those who are suffering from violence.

There is meaning in everything that happens.

last. When things are good in our lives, it is easy to be lulled into the feeling that things will be like this forever. Hard times make us realize that no moment should be taken for granted. Our time on this planet is limited and the feeling of forever is an illusion. Live and love in this moment and may God bless America.

What Freedom Means

Bernie's Take

The crisis in America that began on 9/11—and the events that have followed—make me ask myself once again: Is this what freedom is all about?

Of course, the answer is an emphatic, no! There is a difference between liberty and license. Many people have thrown all rules overboard in the belief that they are free—free to do as they please. But are they? Haven't they merely found themselves victims of a more degrading bondage—the bondage of indecision, instability, anxiety, and fear?

Freedom doesn't mean indifference. What good are strong and agile legs if we don't know in which direction to run? What good are building materials if we don't know what kind of a house to build? What good is our freedom if we don't know how to use it? If we are not free *for* something, we are not really free. The locomotive, for example, is not free to run through a muddy field. However, it is free to travel on tracks. If it thinks that it has the freedom to leave the tracks and make for the woods, there is a mighty wreck. So it is also with us. We have the freedom to manifest the wonderful divine qualities of care and concern for others, but if during times of crisis we feel we have the freedom to take advantage of others, then we, too, are headed for a mighty wreck.

In every crisis God will never baby us by shielding us from pain. But God will lead us through pain, loneliness, frustration, and searching to the strong gentle wisdom that only the Divine One can inspire in us. During these troubled times we will meet countless people starving for kindness, for acceptance, for someone to take them as they are, for someone to stand up for them, for someone to help them overcome the mistrust of themselves and of others. Our Creator walks with us but never offers us a bed of roses. God's way during these times does not necessarily lead us to foreign countries but to such needy places as our own home, our own family, our own city or state. Here we are asked to take time and consider the needs of others, to remember the weakness and loneliness of others, to stop asking how much our friends love us, but whether we love them enough, or to bear in mind the things that others have to bear in their hearts. We will even be introduced to others we have never met before but who need our friendship, example, and help. This, then, is true freedom: the unrestricted ability to make life better for oneself and for others.

So in times of crisis, we should constantly pray, not for easy lives, but to become stronger individuals. We should pray not for tasks equal to our powers, but for powers equal to our tasks. Then every day we shall surely wonder at the richness of our lives and at the zest we have for living. For we will be living our true freedom not for just an hour, not for just a day, not for just a year, but always!

23
Sursum Corda

When I was in Roman Catholic grade school, learning the Latin responses to the Mass was a rite of passage. In the sixth grade, the entire class learned the responses even though only the boys would actually serve at the altar during Mass. Many mornings I sat in the front row during Mass and said the responses silently as my male counterparts recited them out loud.

At one point in the Mass, the priest said, *"Sursum corda"* (Lift up your hearts), and the response was, *"Habemus ad Dominum"* (We have lifted them up to the Lord). The other day those words began ringing in my mind like a half-remembered tune from long ago. Why did they come back and what were they saying to me? As I pondered their meaning in light of my life today, they took on a new significance.

"Lift up your hearts." The word *heart* here means whatever thing, person, or situation is capturing my feelings, thoughts, and attention. To lift up my heart means I have to move my heart from one place to another. Why would I want to move?

There are many times when my heart is in the right place. I am living from my spiritual center. My heart has already been lifted up.

There are other times when my heart needs to move from where it is. When I am stuck in a negative feeling, such as anger, resentment, discouragement, fear, or hatred, I need to move from there. I am not saying that I should deny any of these feelings. I need to recognize them, understand their roots, and then move on. This is what *sursum corda* is all about. It has to do with finding peace of mind. Peace of mind is our divine birthright. As children of a Divine Parent, we have inherited this quality. There is a place within us where God dwells. It is a place of peace, love, and compassion. It is a place of wisdom. We have a right to live our lives from this place. When we dwell in this state of mind and heart we are at peace.

Those of us who have journeyed down the road a bit have all experienced this peace many times in our lives, but perhaps we have not identified it in quite this way. There have been moments in the midst of trauma, difficulties, and loss when we have lifted up our hearts and a peace has settled over us.

Recalling events like these in our lives reminds us that peace of mind can always be ours in any situation. Peace comes from knowing that despite everything that is happening, we are always being taken care of. No matter how difficult the circumstances, nothing lasts forever, but while it is here, we have divine help at hand. We have everything we need to deal with the present crisis or situation.

These thoughts can comfort us in the midst of crisis or trauma, but what about other times, when we feel disgruntled and everything seems to be going wrong? Our peace of mind is destroyed as we find ourselves in the grip of frustration, anger, or fear and we wonder: "How can we ever lift up our hearts under these circumstances?" How do we find our peace of mind again?

We turn again to the principles of spiritual balance that we discussed in earlier chapters. First of all, to lift up your heart means to truly desire to move beyond the negative experience. Sometimes there is a strange satisfaction in wallowing in our negativity, and we really do not want to let go of it. Once you make up your mind to let go of the issue and move on, you are ready to take the next step.

The second step is to ask for help from God, your angels, and your spirit guides. They are always eager to help you move to a place of love and peace in your life.

The next step is to formulate an affirmation that is appropriate for the situation. Find a way to word it that resonates with you. The more precisely it addresses the issue and expresses your own positive insights, the more effective it will be.

Affirmations

I have everything I need to deal with today's challenges.

I am always being taken care of.

My day begins and ends with peace of mind.

The final step is persistence in using the affirmation. Keep saying those words and dwell on their meaning. They will begin to change the feeling and eventually lift up your heart from the shadows of the negative to peace of heart. If you have come this far, you are on the road to success and will be able to answer your own *sursum corda* with a firm, "I have lifted my heart up to the Lord."

The Bigger Picture

Bernie's Take

There isn't a day that goes by in which we do not have the opportunity to "lift up our hearts" to see the bigger picture of what is really going on around us.

For example, in all our recent presidential elections, we have been bombarded with negative ads specifying why this person or that person should not be elected. We begin to get confused, as we try to determine which negative ad is more damaging, and therefore, which person not to vote for. But in lifting up our hearts to see the bigger picture, we realize that we are choosing a person who is going to represent us and our nation. Which candidate do we feel will do the best job of handling the challenges both here and abroad? So we must ask for guidance and help in making such a monumental decision.

Another example is the dilemma within our country and within many faiths over gay and lesbian marriages. Everyone seems to be expressing great fear as to what would happen to "regular" marriages if such gay and lesbian marriages were legalized or solemnized. As a result of this fear, the states are rushing to pass laws forbidding such marriages. The fear is even spawning divisions in many denominations where such unions are permitted.

Once again we have the opportunity to lift up our hearts to see the bigger picture. We need to realize that we are letting *fear* run our lives; fear that gay and lesbian marriages will ruin "real" marriages. Statistics tell us that nearly 50 percent of all regular marriages now end in divorce. Isn't that fear unfounded, since gay and lesbian marriages are just starting to be recognized? There is no way their marriages could be the reason for so many regular marriages failing today. By lifting up our hearts, we can pray for better understanding and acceptance of our brothers and sisters who are also here on this earth to have an intimate relationship with another that leads to personal spiritual growth for oneself and one's partner. After all, our Divine Creator accepts us as we are. Why can't we accept others as they are?

If we are going to keep our balance in these challenging times, we must always remember to "lift up our hearts" and see the bigger picture.

24
Finding Our Niche

For most of us, retirement ushered into our lives a whole new set of activities. No more getting up at 6:00 a.m. every morning. What a joy it was to sleep later and then have a second cup of coffee as we browsed through the newspaper. After that, the day stretched out like a blank sheet of paper. Now we had time to take those trips that we had only dreamed about. There were projects to complete that we had tried to squeeze into our two-week vacation and never finished. It was great being able to play golf when the greens were not so crowded. Now that afternoons were free, joining the ladies' bridge club was a must.

Sometimes we feel we are busier in retirement than when we worked every day. Yet somewhere in those first weeks and months, a question begins to form that invades our comfortable life and leaves us feeling a bit uneasy in spite of all the dreams fulfilled. Is this all there is?

What could possibly be missing in our retirement dream? Through much of this book, we have been talking about spirituality and we believe that a spiritual foundation is certainly necessary. But one of the most important points about spiritual balance has not yet been discussed.

Part of being spiritually balanced is giving service to others. We need to know that we are making a difference, not only in our own lives, but in the lives of others. This lends a sense of meaning and purpose to our later years. Without a sense of service and the opportunity to give back to others, we will always feel that something is missing. Service has been a part of most of our lives, even when we were working. For most of us who incorporated service into our working lives, we simply continued to serve others in our new stage of life.

In the prayer of St. Francis, there is the line, "In giving we receive." Most retirees will tell you that this is true and that they receive more than they give in their particular form of serving.

When considering volunteer work, here are some questions you should ask yourself. What is my passion? What do I like to do? What can I do well? In your service to others you should do what you enjoy. Opportunities abound in almost all areas. You might want to volunteer in a field similar to the one you pursued as a career. As a former teacher, you might want to tutor children on a one-to-one basis. As a retired design artist, being a docent in the local art museum might appeal to you.

On the other hand, maybe you want to get away from the work you did before retirement. Maybe there is an area that you have always wanted to know more about. As a retired teacher, you might enjoy volunteering in a hospital. A former salesperson with a love of animals might choose to serve at the local animal shelter.

Perhaps you will think of a unique way of serving. As I was reading over the alumni news recently, I read about a woman who makes and donates more than one hundred items a month for premature babies. Her much-appreciated volunteer work comes out of her own experience. Her eldest child was born premature and at the time there were no clothes to fit her four-pound daughter. Her donations to an Ohio-based service organization, Touching Little Lives, ensures that other mothers of premature babies will not have the same problem.

Service to others does not have to go beyond one's own family. I know a number of retirees who are caring for their grandchildren on a temporary or permanent basis. They are certainly making a difference in the lives of their children and grandchildren.

As we age, we find our ability to serve limited by various factors. Mobility, difficulty in seeing and hearing, arthritis, and other consequences of an aging body leave us unable to do some of the volunteer work we once enjoyed. But we can always serve.

I am reminded of our ninety-two-year-old friend, Henrietta, who died recently. Her mobility was limited by arthritis of the spine. She was almost blind and could no longer see to read or write, but her mind was still sharp. Up until a few weeks before she died, she continued to serve her elderly friends by making a short telephone call each day to check up on them. After her death, many of her friends mentioned how they missed her daily call. One lady said that Henrietta was her security. She said that, no matter what was happening in her life, she could always call her and get good advice. She doesn't know what she will do without her.

We always have the opportunity to serve, no matter what the state of our bodies. Someone who is bedridden can serve by offering a cheerful smile and an expression of gratitude for what is being done for him. I have heard aides in a nursing home actually argue over which one will take care of a particular patient. Difficulty of care being equal, the argument for or against often depends on the attitude of the patient.

We need to prepare for the time when we may be in this situation. Our bodies may function minimally, but remembering that we are citizens of two worlds will help us gain access to the power of our spirit, not only to help us cope, but to serve others by prayer and meditation.

Recently, I visited the health center of the Sisters of Notre Dame of Namur, the order of nuns to which I belonged. Many sisters there in their seventies, eighties, and nineties are limited in their physical abilities, but they are a powerhouse of spirituality and they know their prayers make a difference.

We do not have to be in a special house of prayer to nurture our spirituality. We can work on our spiritual skills now. We can learn to pray and meditate now. We can store up affirmations for the time when we can no longer see to read or write.

Service will always be one of the anchors in our spiritual balance. As retirees, we have the opportunity to choose the service that we want to perform. We should give some thought to what we do well or enjoy the most when we consider our volunteer services. No matter what the state of our body, we always have the opportunity to serve and know that we can make a difference.

Affirmations

I find those activities in which I can best serve.

I try to be of service to someone each day.

My service makes life easier for others.

Extending a Hand

Bernie's Take

The line "Everybody needs somebody sometime" expresses a well-known fact in both the physical and spiritual worlds. All of us in our younger years have no problem with this as we go about fulfilling our obligations to our employer, our family, and our country. However, by the time retirement age arrives, we may begin to doubt the validity of such a statement. After all those years of long, hard work, we are suddenly encouraged by our employers to retire and enjoy life. Or we notice that our advice no longer seems to be appreciated by our families.

It is at this time that we must realize that we are beginning a new phase in life. A time to cultivate abilities that we never even knew we had. Perhaps you have become quite good at playing golf. Now is the time to develop your special talent as a teacher by volunteering to teach others the nuances of the game. I myself only played golf once in my life and that was with Molly's uncle, who was ninety at the time. He made me practice hitting balls before he would even take me with him on the golf course. His main advice when we actually started heading for the course in his golf cart was this: "Bernie, when you get to be my age, you take advantage of everything you can, even if that means teeing off from the women's tee." He also advised me that we would play nine holes first to see how tired I got. Even though we ended up playing eighteen holes, with me losing a number of his balls, to this day I really appreciate the little tips he so patiently gave me.

If you love being around people, perhaps you might consider volunteering as an aide at a school. You may be surprised at how catching your smile or sense of humor is to those around you. Without realizing it, you are actually becoming more spiritual-minded by your kindness, care, and concern. Others, in turn, will have their own lives enriched because of you.

The best part of one's life is the little nameless, unremembered acts of kindness and helpfulness. Isn't it wonderful to know that when you have found your special niche in life, everyone you touch will always remember the kind look, the warm greeting, or the hand held out in time of need. It is still true that everybody needs somebody sometime.

25
This Moment in Time

The refrain of a song I heard the other day keeps going around in my mind. "Yesterday is history, tomorrow is a mystery, all I have is this moment in time."

What a profound truth spoken in a few words. All that any of us have is this present moment. I began to reflect upon the spiritual significance of this statement and to recognize the spiritual ramifications of this fact.

What does the present moment hold for each of us? This moment is the only time when we can actually do something. We can't do it yesterday and we can plan to do it tomorrow, but now is the only time we can act.

The present moment holds all we need in order to act. It is real time in a way that yesterday or tomorrow can never be. God, who created all time, placed in this moment all the wisdom and divine help we need to act for our good and the good of others. There is also the help we need to be patient and wait when not acting is the best thing we can do.

The present moment is the only place where we can enjoy the full richness of life. Time spent with loved ones takes on a depth of experience when we are truly present. Whether we are supervising our grandchildren on the playground or talking to our spouse, we can multiply the joy of the contact by really being there.

We know the importance of attention in our professional life. How many people have suffered serious consequences from their own inattention to duty or the inattention of others? We see problems created by lack of attention in all walks of life, including medicine, business, education, and public service. A book could probably be written about these types of occurrences, but it is enough to say that many lawsuits—perhaps most—stem from lack of attention in the moment.

Our health could benefit by our attention. Listening to our own bodies has many beneficial consequences. Sometimes it is too late when we arrive at the doctor's to report that nagging abdominal pain that has been with us for months. A superficial breast exam may miss the small lump that can be the start of a more serious problem.

If we are truly present while eating, we can savor the taste of our food. How often do we eat quickly while having a telephone conversation and watching television? How can we really taste the food when we are doing other things while eating?

There is so much beauty in nature we miss if we cannot be present to it—the smell of fresh spring air, the patchwork of colors on the hill made by the fall leaves, the way snow makes patterns on the bushes, a sunset filled with reds, pinks, and purples—all are nature's gifts that can be missed in an ordinary day.

There is not a single action in our lives that cannot be improved with greater presence to the experience, and the marvelous thing is that it does not take any more time to be present. In fact, it may save you time in the end.

It seems like such a simple concept, to do what you are doing, but it is not easy. I have struggled all my life with this very skill. As a child, every year I came home with a report card that had a check next to "Does not concentrate on task at hand." I have had a lifetime of bad habits in this area.

How often I squandered the present moment worrying about the future. How often I spent time reliving a scenario in the past—replaying what I should have said or what I wished "they" would have said. These thoughts are disturbing for me, but it is fruitless to dwell on them. They are lessons I had to learn. All I can do now is to focus on the present moment so that I do not multiply the mistakes of the past.

As we age, it can be difficult to focus on the present because of worries about the future. We look around at our friends and relatives and see people coping with difficult situations as they become less able to care for themselves. We wonder what our special challenges will be as we advance into old age.

We need to think about these things and prepare for them.

Planning for the future can be a present-moment activity. In that moment we have the help that we need to make good plans tailored to our needs. There is a big difference between time spent planning and time spent complaining and worrying about the future. Many hours have been wasted worrying about things in the future that never happened. All we can do is the best we can. Then we have to let it go.

All of us have faced challenges in the past with courage we never thought possible. Often, as a hospital chaplain, I heard people speak of these challenges as they looked back, amazed at the strength they had during those trying times. To me, this is proof that the help and strength, the wisdom and courage needed in future moments, will be there.

I am reminded of the story in the Hebrew Scriptures of the Israelites crossing the desert led by Moses. Each day God provided for their needs. Each morning the group would gather a food called manna that had come down during the night. They were told to gather only what they needed for the day. If they tried to gather more and store it, it would spoil. What they needed was provided each day.

The manna in our lives is the physical, mental, and spiritual help we need to meet the challenges of the present moment. Each morning we can wake up and know without a doubt that our manna will be there. It is provided by a loving and compassionate God. As was done in the desert, so it will be done in all of our "nows."

How do we focus on the present moment? The simple, but not easy answer is moment by moment. Once we experience the power of the present moment, we will want to make it present all the time. Once we know the peace that comes from truly engaging in the moment, whether it is a monumental task or a mundane one, we will always want to be where we are.

Affirmations

I am totally present to this moment.

I let go of the past and the future. I focus on the now.

I enjoy the richness of life in the present moment.

The Power of the Present

Bernie's Take

How true it is that if we can learn to stay in the present moment, we will be surprised at what we can accomplish.

When I was a hospital chaplain, one of the doctors told me this story about what a little six-year-old girl was able to achieve. I would like to share it with you.

Unlike other little girls, Judy (the name I will give her) was unable to walk or run due to some malfunction in her leg muscles. Her doctor decided to try to correct this with surgery. After arriving in the operating room, Judy was told by the nurses that she was going to go to sleep. She immediately decided to say her night prayers. From her bed, she prayed for mommy, daddy, her brothers and sisters. "Please, God," she continued, "help the doctor and nurses make me walk again." Her prayers finished, she laid back down. The surgery was performed.

A few days later the doctor entered her room and was greeted with the question, "Can I walk and run now?"

"Judy," the doctor began, "I don't know yet. But something very good happened because of your operation. I want to tell you about it. I was away from God and my church for twenty-five years. That morning as I saw you pray for me, I decided to come back to God and my church. This I have done and I intend to remain with God and my church the rest of my life. So, thank you, Judy, for praying for me."

I recall this true story because I think it illustrates the wonderful truth that if we choose to live neither in the past nor in the future but only in the now, we will be astounded by the unimaginable and unforeseen good that we will accomplish.

26
Creating a Spiritual Holiday

It's that time of year again—one that stirs emotions and elicits a variety of responses. For those of the Jewish faith, it is called Hanukkah. For Christians, it is called Christmas. Some of us complain because there is so much to be done and so little time to do it. We feel tired before we even begin. How do you cope with all the cards to address, the special foods to make, the decorating to do, and the gifts to buy?

Others simply do not have the physical strength to prepare for festivities. They feel regret and sadness that they can no longer do what they used to do. Limitations of mobility, sight, and hearing leave them outside the preparations for this busy holiday season.

As I approach this time of year, a deep desire wells up within me, and perhaps in many of you, to really have a spiritual holiday. I look back with nostalgia on a very special time in my life when that was possible. My first year as a novice sister was one dedicated entirely to prayer and religious study. We had no concerns about parties, cards, gift giving, job, or family. We were able to immerse ourselves in the spirit of the Advent and Christmas season. Unfortunately, at eighteen years of age, I was unable to appreciate this wonderful opportunity.

I missed the parties, gift buying, decorating, and, of course, I missed my family and friends whom we did not see or communicate with during that time. Instead of focusing on my new life and opportunities, I was focusing on what was missing from my life. Christmas carols and decorations all waited until Christmas Eve. On Christmas and the following days, we experienced the fullness of the season when cards and gifts were received, and friends and family came for a visit.

Once I left the convent and engaged again in the busy preholiday festivities, I often looked back somewhat enviously upon those quiet, peaceful days when I was in training to become a nun. Over the years, I have tried to find a way to infuse the "spiritual" in the holiday season in spite of all that had to be done. It is only recently that I have discovered that a spiritual celebration must be found not in spite of the busy holiday activities, but within those very activities themselves.

The first job we usually tackle here at home is the Christmas letter and cards we send out each year. This is my first "moan and groan" chore, as my hand becomes tired writing and my eyes cross looking at the more than one hundred addresses that need to be copied. A small attitude adjustment within has converted this chore into a prayer. Now, as I write each person, I hold love and a prayer for their good in my heart.

The same is true for shopping. If I look upon gift giving as an opportunity to give to others as I have received in my life, then this leaves me with much to think about. This is not simply an exchange of gifts between family and friends. It is an opportunity to give to those who have so generously given to me. As I look for just the right gift, I hold a prayer for this person in my heart. When I do this, there is no room for "moan and groan," too.

When we think of holiday decorations, whether on a Christmas tree or in our homes, they are traditionally bright and colorful. They sparkle, glow, glisten, and shine. The magic of their beauty adds an otherworldly feeling to our homes, streets, and neighborhoods. Perhaps we are meant to be reminded, at least once a year, that there is a bright and beautiful world that awaits us at the end of our earthly journey.

Light seems to be a special symbol of this holiday season. Whether we light the candles for Hanukkah or the lights on our Christmas tree, the darkness of the winter is brightened by the holiday lights and we are reminded that a light always shines, even in the darkest corners of our lives. Every light is a symbol of the light of God's love that is constantly there for all of us.

We cannot forget that we, who are God's children, carry the divine spark within us. We are lights for one another. Not only do we need to let our light shine, but we also need to recognize the light in the others around us. The menorah bright with lights can remind us of the effect when we all let our light shine.

To me, music has always been the language of heaven. Holiday music has the power to remind us of the spiritual significance of this time of year. From the magnificent *Hallelujah Chorus* to the peaceful *Silent Night,* the holiday season is celebrated in concerts everywhere.

Everything we do and see in the holiday season has a spiritual message. Perhaps we can make it a habit as that season arrives each year, to pause for a few moments and reflect upon the meaning of what we are doing. Whether it is addressing cards or buying gifts, decorating the house or lighting candles, the holiday can be a spiritual experience for all of us.

Affirmations

As I prepare for the holiday season, I find the spiritual meaning in my activities.

All that glows and glistens reminds me of the unseen spiritual gifts of God.

I am a loving light to all at this season.

Accepting Gifts Graciously

Bernie's Take

There comes a time, usually at the end of each year, when we need to forget the hustle and bustle of everyday living and create a special spiritual holiday—a time for living in the joy of the moment. For those of us of the Christian faith, this time is called Christmas; for those of the Jewish faith it is known as Hanukkah.

These are wonderful times of giving and receiving presents. They convey special meaning. "I love you," "I miss you," "I want you to be happy." Gifts seek to please, to surprise, to amuse. They recall good times in the past and indicate hopes for the future.

Besides physical gifts that we can give or receive, there are other gifts that may not come gift-wrapped, but that are just as important at this time of the year. Such gifts may be charitable deeds, such as cleaning the home of a senior citizen, decorating someone's home, or volunteering to cook the special meal appropriate to one's beliefs.

As enjoyable as it is to give these "unwrapped" gifts at this time, it is also important for us to accept gifts and services graciously. This is easier said than done. Why? Maybe we feel as though we cannot repay the gift. Or perhaps we don't want to become indebted to the giver.

Yet everyone must accept help of some sort at some time. And the key to accepting these gifts graciously is to realize that someone is sharing through love; and sharing is both giving and receiving. You cannot have one without the other. So it is just as blessed to receive as it is to give; the two are so closely related. If we learn to openly acknowledge and accept the help that we have received, we can be sure that we will be growing spiritually. We will have learned the true secret of being able to give as well as receive. We will have created a truly spiritual holiday.

27
Moving On

The nest is empty now, but for a number of weeks we enjoyed the presence of a pair of finches who decided to nest in the feeder outside our kitchen window.

The process began with a careful examination of the site by both mother and father bird. It must have received quick approval because it was not long before twigs and grass were flown in and used to fashion a nest where the mother bird took up residence. I was amazed to see the father bird bring her food, while she faithfully sat on the nest. Not only did he bring food, but as he left he would pick up her droppings with his beak and carry them off. Imagine a male that voluntarily takes out the trash!

It wasn't long before four bald heads and four very large mouths were bobbing above the rim of the nest. Then both parents made frequent trips just to keep the family fed. One morning I noticed that those bald heads were getting feathers and I saw them flexing their wings. I knew it wouldn't be long before we could hang a

For Rent sign on the feeder. I went to the store that day, and when I returned, the nest was empty.

I felt sad to see them gone and knew I would miss watching their progress every day. It reminded me that this is what life is about—moving on. Nothing really stays the same and when we try to hold onto the present moment, it slips through our fingers.

As we look back over our lives, we can see a pattern of moving on. We moved from babyhood to grade school, from grade school to high school, and then to college or work. Raising a family and experiencing our own empty nest was part of our progress in life.

At each "moving on" in our lives, we felt both sadness and excitement. The tearful good-byes gave way to a new time in life. Lately, those times of moving on, for many of us, have not been accompanied by the excitement we once felt. The "new time in life" for us may seem more like the end of the road.

In the early stages of our lives, our time was spent acquiring things and inviting others into our lives. We acquired a house, furnishings, a car, and many other material possessions. A spouse, children, friends shared life with us. At a certain time our life peaked, as it were, and then we began a new phase in life—the phase of not only moving on but of letting go. Our children leave home to start lives of their own. We sell our home and dispose of many of our furnishings. We move into an apartment or retirement center. Our body itself begins to show signs of wear and tear. At this time in life, it is not unusual to pick up the newspaper and see the names of our friends and relatives in the obituary column.

Looked at from a purely material point of view, this can be a disheartening time in life. But for many of us it is not disheartening at all because we have stored up treasures that neither rust nor time can destroy. As we age, it is important to recognize and cherish these treasures. We need to draw comfort and strength from their presence in our lives.

One of those treasures is the wisdom we have gained from our life experience. As we look back over our lives, we can identify things we have learned from both our failures and our successes. We can pinpoint events in our lives that were our teachers and had a profound effect on our lives. At times we have tried to share this wisdom with the younger ones, only to discover that they need to learn from their own experience.

Another treasure is the relationships that we have forged. There are the warm fuzzy relationships of children, grandchildren, and great grandchildren. Many rejoice in seeing the family bloodline continuing. We are a part of all those children. Hopefully, each of us can relish the love relationships of spouses or partners and friends that have enriched our lives and left us with cherished memories. There are others whose relationships have been hard on us. Even from these, we can draw lessons that contribute to our wisdom.

Over the years we have developed talents and gifts. Even though we may not be using them at this moment, they are a part of us and should always be viewed as a source of achievement. Our ninety-two-year-old friend Henrietta worked in a factory most of her life. One particular job was done with drill bits that cost $100 apiece. Various workers tried to do the job, but most ended up breaking the drill bits. The boss put Henrietta on the job and she finished the entire job without breaking one bit. Even at ninety-two, she could tell the story with pride and feel a sense of accomplishment.

With all these treasures, we build a sense of self. Old age is not the time to be humble and modest about our achievements. If we cannot acknowledge them to others, at least we need to recognize them ourselves.

For me, personally, and I suspect for many others, the greatest treasure we have at this time in life, and as we continue to age, is spirituality. This is the treasure that helps us see beyond the challenges of life—the pain, loss, frustration, and heartbreak—that is necessarily a part of our journey on this earth.

This is the treasure that gives us a peek into the future. Our spirituality helps us see the meaning in all the moments in life, especially those that seem most unproductive.

This is the treasure that helps us see beyond the door of death and realize that the best is yet to be. We see death as a returning home to a place that is familiar. It will be a grand reunion with God and those who have gone before us. As we move on, we will find that we are very much ourselves with our memories, our accomplishments, our skills, and our relationships intact. Here we will have the chance to evaluate the life we lived while on earth and to move in new directions of learning and growth.

As we contemplate moving on to the next stage in our existence, we can do so with all the confidence and excitement that this is the best move yet.

Affirmations

I accept change as a necessary part of life.

I gather the wisdom of my life and rejoice in it.

I build a strong spiritual foundation that will see me through the door of death.

Embracing New Challenges

Bernie's Take

Not only was "Those Were the Days" a popular song a while back, but it was probably the theme song of many of our lives. We seem to be constantly looking back to those good old days when men had their weekend mechanic's license to tune up their own car, women hung clothes out on the line to dry, and children used their imagination to make up games to pass the lazy days of summer.

Then suddenly we began to awaken to the beat of the song "The Times They Are A-Changing." Much to our surprise, we even found ourselves dancing through life to the theme song of *The Jeffersons* TV show "Movin' On Up." And that is where we have been ever since—moving on up!

The important lesson of our earth-school curriculum is that all of us must realize that we are not to remain satisfied with the way things are. We certainly cannot remain a senior in high school forever, but must go on to the next step in life—be that college, a job, the military, or marriage, to name but a few. It means that we must begin to constantly challenge ourselves by letting go of past experiences, insights, and lessons so that we can be open to the wonderful new adventures, discoveries, and information we are about to experience. Otherwise, our lives will become dull and void of any excitement.

If this is true of the material world in which we live, likewise, it is true of the spiritual world in which we live. We must begin to learn not to become so attached to our own idea of the way things should be that we close our minds to gaining new insights into what the spirit world is really like.

Some time ago, I heard someone tell the ancient story about a father who was out of town on business. An enemy came and burned down all the houses and killed the people of the town. The father returned to find his home in ashes and discovered a few bones that he believed to be those of his son. He gathered them up and laid them in a place of honor in the new home he built over the spot where his previous home had been. One night he heard a pounding on his door. When asked who it was, he received the answer: "It's your son!"

"Go away," the father said. "My son is dead."

After several nights of pounding and the father's constant begging him to go away, the son sadly left, never to return. Because the father was not open to the idea that his son might have escaped from the fire, he spent the rest of his life believing that his son had died in the fire.

So you see it is important for us to always be willing to "move on" and be open to new ideas, new insights, and new truths. Otherwise, we, too, will go through life never getting to know the real truth.

Afterword

This book was designed to help you understand and utilize the power of spirituality in your life as you grow older. Part I, "The Ground on Which We Stand," began with the recognition that you are a citizen of two worlds. Ways were suggested to help you identify with your spiritual nature, just as you identified with your physical self. You learned to recognize the characteristics of both ego and spirit in your life and the importance of allowing spirit or soul to be in control of your decisions and actions.

You were invited to take another look at who God is in your life and to explore your relationship with your divine Father/Mother God. You were reminded of other spiritual beings—angels and saints and spirit guides—who have been sent to you to help you remember and fulfill your spiritual nature and mission here on earth.

You became acquainted with the many spiritual tools you have to facilitate your spiritual growth while here on earth. You saw the power of the universal laws, your thoughts, and your own precious free will in your spiritual destiny. You observed that death is more an entrance into a new life than an end to this one.

In Part II, "Spirituality—Day by Day," you saw the fundamentals of spirituality operating in everyday situations. It led you to reflect with spiritual perspective on such subjects as war and peace, the gifts of nature, prayer and meditation, gratitude, serving others, the challenges of aging, the importance of the present moment, and other issues we all face in daily life.

You saw how spirituality can be lived every day in both the big and small events of life. It can run like a thread through the day, stitching each event with meaning into the patchwork of the day, until the quilt of your life is finally complete.

Listed on the following pages are the affirmations that were included in each chapter. They are a most effective tool that can be used every day to spiritually enrich your retirement years.

Affirmations

I am a spiritual being with a physical body that is temporary and a spiritual body that will live forever.

My spiritual body is who I really am.

I will pass through the door of death with my eyes wide open and all my faculties intact.

I see my spiritual body radiating light and love.

I see my physical body pierced through with the light of my spirit.

My spiritual body and my physical body work together for good.

Every day I quickly become aware of my negative emotions and I deal with them effectively.

I let go of all past hurts and send peace and love to those who have hurt me.

I send love to those I have deliberately or unknowingly hurt. I ask God to bless them.

I open my heart and mind to the presence of the true God.

God is a loving Mother/Father. I respond as a loving child.

I let go of all false ideas of God in my mind and I embrace the true God in my heart.

I have everything I need to meet the challenges I face today.

Good things are always coming to me.

Every day I move closer to my spiritual goals.

My angels and guides are always with me. I am never alone.

Angels and guides protect me against all physical and spiritual dangers.

Angels and guides walk with me today and lead me along the right paths.

I grow every day in my understanding of the spiritual laws and how they apply to my life.

My eyes are opened to the working of the spiritual laws in the lives of those around me.

The law of cause and effect frees me from any desire for revenge against another person.

I am always aware of the power of my thoughts and words.

I monitor my thoughts carefully, so that in my thoughts and actions I will do no harm.

I use my thoughts and words to spread peace in the world.

I accept the responsibility that accompanies my free will.

I always strive to recognize the moment of choice before I make a decision.

I make choices in my life that are good for me and for others.

I accept my aging as a sign of a better life to come.

Before I die, I find and repay debts owed.

My death is a joyful homecoming, uniting me with my loved ones who have passed on.

I focus my total attention on the present moment.

I meet the Holy in every moment of my life.

I claim the opportunity to grow spiritually in every moment of the day.

I let go of any negative conjectures for the future.

I open my mind to the positive possibilities for our world.

The loving presence of the Holy helps me envision a happy and fulfilling future.

I recognize the gifts in the hardships that come my way.

In the midst of adversity, I have faith that a gift is there for me.

I am grateful for the gifts present in the difficulties of my life.

In sunny days and foggy days, I trust in God.

Every time of trial has a spiritual lesson. I look for it.

I live in the present moment.

God's smile is always with me.

I share the smile of God with others.

I turn toward God and embrace the love that is offered me.

Springtime immerses me in the beauty of the Creator.

I am open to the spiritual lessons nature has to teach me.

I accept my aging as a natural preparation for the next step in my journey.

I let go of any negativity in myself that does not lead to peace.

I recognize and emulate the peacemakers I see every day.

I am a peacemaker in my family, my community, and my world.

As my body ages, I participate in life as fully as possible.

I do not let age serve as an excuse for whining and complaining.

I look for lessons in courage and perseverance from my furry and feathered friends.

I open my mind and my heart to the presence of the spiritual gifts around me.

I claim the spiritual gifts available to me.

I am grateful to God for the many material and spiritual blessings in my life.

Today I will live from my spiritual center.

There is always more than one way of looking at my life.

I always have a choice in the way I deal with problems in my life.

I create a special place of worship within that is right for me.

As I pray, a sacred space opens around me.

As I open my mind and heart in prayer, I am surrounded by a holy light.

God's support is always present in the hard times of my life.

I send light and love today to those who are suffering from violence.

There is meaning in everything that happens.

I have everything I need to deal with today's challenges.

I am always being taken care of.

My day begins and ends with peace of mind.

I find those activities in which I can best serve.

I try to be of service to someone each day.

My service makes life easier for others.

I am totally present to this moment.

I let go of the past and the future. I focus on the now.

I enjoy the richness of life in the present moment.

As I prepare for the holiday season, I find the spiritual meaning in my activities.

All that glows and glistens reminds me of the unseen spiritual gifts of God.

I am a loving light to all at this season.

I accept change as a necessary part of life.

I gather the wisdom of my life and rejoice in it.

I build a strong spiritual foundation that will see me through the door of death.

Acknowledgments

We are grateful to our family and friends for their supportive interest and encouragement during the writing of this manuscript.

Special thanks:

To Jon Sweeney, associate publisher of SkyLight Paths, for his suggestion that we coauthor this book.

To Maura Shaw, our editor at SkyLight Paths, for her expert advice and guidance in the preparation of this manuscript.

To Shelly Angers for her enthusiasm and time invested in publicizing this work.

To the many fine people at SkyLight Paths who worked behind the scenes to make this book possible.

To the staff of Antioch Writer's Workshop, Yellow Springs, Ohio, for their valuable information about the craft of writing.

Most of all, to the One who makes all things possible, and to our angels and spirit guides who have been around us, especially during the writing of this book, whispering inspiration and giving encouragement.

About SKYLIGHT PATHS Publishing

SkyLight Paths Publishing is creating a place where people of different spiritual traditions come together for challenge and inspiration, a place where we can help each other understand the mystery that lies at the heart of our existence.

Through spirituality, our religious beliefs are increasingly becoming a part of our lives—rather than *apart* from our lives. While many of us may be more interested than ever in spiritual growth, we may be less firmly planted in traditional religion. Yet, we do want to deepen our relationship to the sacred, to learn from our own as well as from other faith traditions, and to practice in new ways.

SkyLight Paths sees both believers and seekers as a community that increasingly transcends traditional boundaries of religion and denomination—people wanting to learn from each other, *walking together, finding the way.*

We at SkyLight Paths take great care to produce beautiful books that present meaningful spiritual content in a form that reflects the art of making high quality books. Therefore, we want to acknowledge those who contributed to the production of this book.

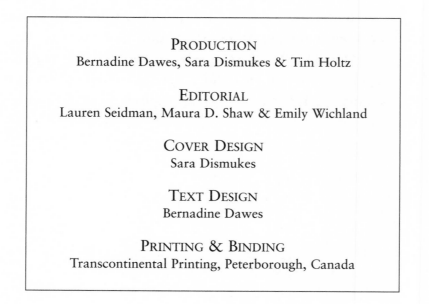

PRODUCTION
Bernadine Dawes, Sara Dismukes & Tim Holtz

EDITORIAL
Lauren Seidman, Maura D. Shaw & Emily Wichland

COVER DESIGN
Sara Dismukes

TEXT DESIGN
Bernadine Dawes

PRINTING & BINDING
Transcontinental Printing, Peterborough, Canada

Other Interesting Books—Spirituality

Journeys of Simplicity: *Traveling Light with Thomas Merton, Bashō, Edward Abbey, Annie Dillard & Others*
by *Philip Harnden*

Offers vignettes of forty "travelers" and the few ordinary things they carried with them—from place to place, from day to day, from birth to death. What Thoreau took to Walden Pond. What Thomas Merton packed for his final trip to Asia. What Annie Dillard keeps in her writing tent. What an impoverished cook served M. F. K. Fisher for dinner. Much more.

"'How much should I carry with me?' is the quintessential question for any journey, especially the journey of life. Herein you'll find sage, sly, wonderfully subversive advice." —Bill McKibben, author of *The End of Nature* and *Enough*

5 x 7¼, 128 pp, HC, ISBN 1-893361-76-4 **$16.95**

What Matters: *Spiritual Nourishment for Head and Heart*
by *Frederick Franck*

Savor what truly matters in your own life.

This elegantly simple book of reflections presents the rich harvest of a lifetime of thinking, feeling, and seeing by an artist whose vital spirituality has inspired hundreds of thousands of readers and students through his art, books, and workshops. The pithy, sometimes humorous, always wise contemplations reveal Franck's lifelong confrontation with the human in himself and others.

5 x 7¼, 144 pp, 50+ b/w illus., HC, ISBN 1-59473-013-X **$16.99**

Spiritually Incorrect: *Finding God in All the* Wrong *Places*
by *Dan Wakefield*; Illus. by *Marian DelVecchio*

Spirituality is full of rules. You need to find your own way straight through them.

Award-winning author Dan Wakefield dares to ask the risky (and sometimes hilarious) questions about spirituality. His insightful reflections break down the barriers that lie in the way of spiritual fulfillment, showing you that it's possible—and imperative—for you to discover a rewarding spiritual life that fits your own personality, your own path.

5½ x 8½, 192 pp, b/w illus., HC, ISBN 1-893361-88-8 **$21.95**

Or phone, fax, mail or e-mail to: SKYLIGHT PATHS Publishing
Sunset Farm Offices, Route 4 • P.O. Box 237 • Woodstock, Vermont 05091
Tel: (802) 457-4000 • Fax: (802) 457-4004 • www.skylightpaths.com
Credit card orders: (800) 962-4544 (8:30AM–5:30PM ET Monday–Friday)
Generous discounts on quantity orders. SATISFACTION GUARANTEED. Prices subject to change.

Spiritual Biography

The Life of Evelyn Underhill: *An Intimate Portrait of the Groundbreaking Author of* Mysticism
by *Margaret Cropper;* Foreword by *Dana Greene*

Evelyn Underhill was a passionate writer and teacher who wrote elegantly on mysticism, worship, and devotional life. This is the story of how she made her way toward spiritual maturity, from her early days of agnosticism to the years when her influence was felt throughout the world. 6 x 9, 288 pp, 5 b/w photos, Quality PB, ISBN 1-893361-70-5 **$18.95**

Zen Effects: *The Life of Alan Watts*
by *Monica Furlong*

The first and only full-length biography of one of the most charismatic spiritual leaders of the twentieth century—now back in print!

Through his widely popular books and lectures, Alan Watts (1915–1973) did more to introduce Eastern philosophy and religion to Western minds than any figure before or since. Here is the only biography of this charismatic figure, who served as Zen teacher, Anglican priest, lecturer, academic, entertainer, a leader of the San Francisco renaissance, and author of more than 30 books, including *The Way of Zen, Psychotherapy East and West* and *The Spirit of Zen.*
6 x 9, 264 pp, Quality PB, ISBN 1-893361-32-2 **$16.95**

Simone Weil: *A Modern Pilgrimage*
by *Robert Coles*

The extraordinary life of the spiritual philosopher who's been called both saint and madwoman.

The French writer and philosopher Simone Weil (1906–1943) devoted her life to a search for God—while avoiding membership in organized religion. Robert Coles' intriguing study of Weil details her short, eventful life, and is an insightful portrait of the beloved and controversial thinker whose life and writings influenced many (from T. S. Eliot to Adrienne Rich to Albert Camus), and continue to inspire seekers everywhere.
6 x 9, 208 pp, Quality PB, ISBN 1-893361-34-9 **$16.95**

Mahatma Gandhi: *His Life and Ideas*
by *Charles F. Andrews;* Foreword by *Dr. Arun Gandhi*

An intimate biography of one of the greatest social and religious reformers of the modern world.

Examines from a contemporary Christian activist's point of view the religious ideas and political dynamics that influenced the birth of the peaceful resistance movement, the primary tool that Gandhi and the people of his homeland would use to gain India its freedom from British rule. An ideal introduction to the life and life's work of this great spiritual leader.
6 x 9, 336 pp, 5 b/w photos, Quality PB, ISBN 1-893361-89-6 **$18.95**

Spiritual Retreats

Lighting the Lamp of Wisdom: *A Week Inside a Yoga Ashram*
by *John Ittner*; Foreword by *Dr. David Frawley*

This insider's guide to Hindu spiritual life takes you into a typical week of retreat inside a yoga ashram to demystify the experience and show you what to expect from your own visit. Includes a discussion of worship services, meditation and yoga classes, chanting and music, work practice, and more.
6 x 9, 192 pp, b/w photographs, Quality PB, ISBN 1-893361-52-7 **$15.95**;
HC, ISBN 1-893361-37-3 **$24.95**

Waking Up: *A Week Inside a Zen Monastery*
by *Jack Maguire*; Foreword by *John Daido Loori, Roshi*

An essential guide to what it's like to spend a week inside a Zen Buddhist monastery.
6 x 9, 224 pp, b/w photographs, Quality PB, ISBN 1-893361-55-1 **$16.95**;
HC, ISBN 1-893361-13-6 **$21.95**

Making a Heart for God: *A Week Inside a Catholic Monastery*
by *Dianne Aprile*; Foreword by *Brother Patrick Hart*, OCSO

This essential guide to experiencing life in a Catholic monastery takes you to the Abbey of Gethsemani—the Trappist monastery in Kentucky that was home to author Thomas Merton—to explore the details. "More balanced and informative than the popular *The Cloister Walk* by Kathleen Norris." —*Choice: Current Reviews for Academic Libraries*
6 x 9, 224 pp, b/w photographs, Quality PB, ISBN 1-893361-49-7 **$16.95**;
HC, ISBN 1-893361-14-4 **$21.95**

Come and Sit: *A Week Inside Meditation Centers*
by *Marcia Z. Nelson*; Foreword by *Wayne Teasdale*

The insider's guide to meditation in a variety of different spiritual traditions. Traveling through Buddhist, Hindu, Christian, Jewish, and Sufi traditions, this essential guide takes you to different meditation centers to meet the teachers and students and learn about the practices, demystifying the meditation experience.
6 x 9, 224 pp, b/w photographs, Quality PB, ISBN 1-893361-35-7 **$16.95**

Interspirituality

A Walk with Four Spiritual Guides: *Krishna, Buddha, Jesus, and Ramakrishna*
by *Andrew Harvey*

Andrew Harvey's warm and personal introduction to each guide offers his own experiences of learning from their wisdom.

Krishna, Buddha, Jesus, Ramakrishna: four of the world's most interesting and challenging spiritual masters. The core of their most important teachings—along with annotations from expert scholars and introductions from Andrew Harvey, one of the great spiritual thinkers of our time—now are all in one beautiful volume.

5½ x 8½, 192 pp, 10 b/w photos & illus., Hardcover, ISBN 1-893361-73-X **$21.95**

The Alphabet of Paradise: *An A–Z of Spirituality for Everyday Life*
by *Howard Cooper*

"An extraordinary book." —Karen Armstrong

One of the most eloquent new voices in spirituality, Howard Cooper takes us on a journey of discovery—into ourselves and into the past—to find the signposts that can help us live more meaningful lives. In twenty-six engaging chapters—from A to Z—Cooper spiritually illuminates the subjects of daily life, using an ancient Jewish mystical method of interpretation that reveals both the literal and more allusive meanings of each. Topics include: Awe, Bodies, Creativity, Dreams, Emotions, Sports, and more.

5 x 7¾, 224 pp, Quality PB, ISBN 1-893361-80-2 **$16.95**

Daughters of the Desert: *Tales of Remarkable Women from Christian, Jewish, and Muslim Traditions*
by *Claire Rudolf Murphy, Meghan Nuttall Sayres, Mary Cronk Farrell, Sarah Conover,* and *Betsy Wharton*

Breathes new life into the old tales of our female ancestors in faith.

The authors use traditional scriptural passages as their starting points, then with vivid detail fill in historical context and place. Chapters reveal the voices of Sarah, Hagar, Huldah, Esther, Salome, Mary Magdalene, Lydia, Khadija, Fatima, and many more. Historical fiction ideal for readers of all ages. 5½ x 8½, 192 pp, HC, ISBN 1-893361-72-1 **$19.95**

Bede Griffiths: *An Introduction to His Interspiritual Thought*
by *Wayne Teasdale*

The first in-depth study of Bede Griffiths' contemplative experience and thought.

Wayne Teasdale, a longtime personal friend and student of Griffiths, creates in this intimate portrait an intriguing view into the beliefs and life of this champion of interreligious acceptance and harmony. Explains key terms that form the basis of Griffiths' contemplative understanding, and the essential characteristics of his theology as they relate to the Hindu and Christian traditions.

6 x 9, 288 pp, Quality PB, ISBN 1-893361-77-2 **$18.95**

Spiritual Practice

The Sacred Art of Bowing: *Preparing to Practice*

by *Andi Young*

This informative and inspiring introduction to bowing—and related spiritual practices—shows you how to do it, why it's done, and what spiritual benefits it has to offer. Incorporates interviews, personal stories, illustrations of bowing in practice, advice on how you can incorporate bowing into your daily life, and how bowing can deepen spiritual understanding.

5½ x 8½, 128 pp, b/w illus., Quality PB, ISBN 1-893361-82-9 **$14.95**

Praying with Our Hands
Twenty-One Practices of Embodied Prayer from the World's Spiritual Traditions

by *Jon M. Sweeney;* Photographs by *Jennifer J. Wilson;*
Foreword by *Mother Tessa Bielecki;* Afterword by *Taitetsu Unno, PhD*

A spiritual guidebook for bringing prayer into our bodies.

This inspiring book of reflections and accompanying photographs shows us twenty-one simple ways of using our hands to speak to God, to enrich our devotion and ritual. All express the various approaches of the world's religious traditions to bringing the body into worship. Spiritual traditions represented include Anglican, Sufi, Zen, Roman Catholic, Yoga, Shaker, Hindu, Jewish, Pentecostal, Eastern Orthodox, and many others.

8 x 8, 96 pp, 22 duotone photographs, Quality PB, ISBN 1-893361-16-0 **$16.95**

The Sacred Art of Listening: *Forty Reflections for Cultivating a Spiritual Practice*

by *Kay Lindahl;* Illustrations by *Amy Schnapper*

More than ever before, we need to embrace the skills and practice of listening. You will learn to: Speak clearly from your heart • Communicate with courage and compassion • Heighten your awareness for deep listening • Enhance your ability to listen to people with different belief systems. 8 x 8, 160 pp, Illus., Quality PB, ISBN 1-893361-44-6 **$16.99**

Labyrinths from the Outside In: *Walking to Spiritual Insight—A Beginner's Guide*

by *Donna Schaper* and *Carole Ann Camp*

The user-friendly, interfaith guide to making and using labyrinths—
for meditation, prayer, and celebration.

Labyrinth walking is a spiritual exercise *anyone* can do. This accessible guide unlocks the mysteries of the labyrinth for all of us, providing ideas for using the labyrinth walk for prayer, meditation, and celebrations to mark the most important moments in life. Includes instructions for making a labyrinth of your own and finding one in your area.

6 x 9, 208 pp, b/w illus. and photographs, Quality PB, ISBN 1-893361-18-7 **$16.95**

SkyLight Illuminations Series
Andrew Harvey, series editor

Offers today's spiritual seeker an enjoyable entry into the great classic texts of the world's spiritual traditions. Each classic is presented in an accessible translation, with facing pages of guided commentary from experts, giving you the keys you need to understand the history, context, and meaning of the text. This series enables readers of all backgrounds to experience and understand classic spiritual texts directly, and to make them a part of their lives. Andrew Harvey writes the foreword to each volume, an insightful, personal introduction to each classic.

Bhagavad Gita: *Annotated & Explained*
Translation by *Shri Purohit Swami*; Annotation by *Kendra Crossen Burroughs*

"The very best Gita for first-time readers." —Ken Wilber

Millions of people turn daily to India's most beloved holy book, whose universal appeal has made it popular with non-Hindus and Hindus alike. This edition introduces you to the characters, explains references and philosophical terms, shares the interpretations of famous spiritual leaders and scholars, and more.
5½ x 8½, 192 pp, Quality PB, ISBN 1-893361-28-4 **$16.95**

The Way of a Pilgrim: *Annotated & Explained*
Translation and annotation by *Gleb Pokrovsky*

This classic of Russian spirituality is the delightful account of one man who sets out to learn the prayer of the heart—also known as the "Jesus prayer"—and how the practice transforms his life.
5½ x 8½, 160 pp, Illus., Quality PB, ISBN 1-893361-31-4 **$14.95**

The Gospel of Thomas: *Annotated & Explained*
Translation and annotation by *Stevan Davies*

Discovered in 1945, this collection of aphoristic sayings sheds new light on the origins of Christianity and the intriguing figure of Jesus, portraying the Kingdom of God as a present fact about the world, rather than a future promise or future threat. This edition guides you through the text with annotations that focus on the meaning of the sayings.
5½ x 8½, 192 pp, Quality PB, ISBN 1-893361-45-4 **$16.95**

Rumi and Islam: *Selections from His Stories, Poems, and Discourses—Annotated & Explained*
Translation and annotation by *Ibrahim Gamard*

Offers a new way of thinking about Rumi's poetry. Ibrahim Gamard focuses on Rumi's place within the Sufi tradition of Islam, providing you with insight into the mystical side of the religion—one that has love of God at its core and sublime wisdom teachings as its pathways.
5½ x 8½, 240 pp, Quality PB, ISBN 1-59473-002-4 **$15.99**

SkyLight Illuminations Series
Andrew Harvey, series editor

Zohar: *Annotated & Explained*
Translation and annotation by *Daniel C. Matt*
The cornerstone text of Kabbalah.

The best-selling author of *The Essential Kabbalah* brings together in one place the most important teachings of the *Zohar*, the canonical text of Jewish mystical tradition. Guides you step by step through the midrash, mystical fantasy, and Hebrew scripture that make up the *Zohar*, explaining the inner meanings in facing-page commentary. Ideal for readers without any prior knowledge of Jewish mysticism.

5½ x 8½, 176 pp, Quality PB, ISBN 1-893361-51-9 **$15.99**

Selections from the Gospel of Sri Ramakrishna: *Annotated & Explained*
Translation by *Swami Nikhilananda*; Annotation by *Kendra Crossen Burroughs*
The words of India's greatest example of God-consciousness and mystical ecstasy in recent history.

Introduces the fascinating world of the Indian mystic and the universal appeal of his message that has inspired millions of devotees for more than a century. Selections from the original text and insightful yet unobtrusive commentary highlight the most important and inspirational teachings. Ideal for readers without any prior knowledge of Hinduism.

5½ x 8½, 240 pp, b/w photographs, Quality PB, ISBN 1-893361-46-2 **$16.95**

Dhammapada: *Annotated & Explained*
Translation by *Max Müller* and revised by *Jack Maguire*; Annotation by *Jack Maguire*
The classic of Buddhist spiritual practice.

The Dhammapada—words spoken by the Buddha himself over 2,500 years ago—is notoriously difficult to understand for the first-time reader. Now you can experience it with understanding even if you have no previous knowledge of Buddhism. Enlightening facing-page commentary explains all the names, terms, and references, giving you deeper insight into the text.

5½ x 8½, 160 pp, b/w photographs, Quality PB, ISBN 1-893361-42-X **$14.95**

Hasidic Tales: *Annotated & Explained*
Translation and annotation by *Rabbi Rami Shapiro*
The legendary tales of the impassioned Hasidic rabbis.

The allegorical quality of Hasidic tales can be perplexing. Here, they are presented as stories rather than parables, making them accessible and meaningful. Each demonstrates the spiritual power of unabashed joy, offers lessons for leading a holy life, and reminds us that the Divine can be found in the everyday. Annotations explain theological concepts, introduce major characters, and clarify references unfamiliar to most readers.

5½ x 8½, 240 pp, Quality PB, ISBN 1-893361-86-1 **$16.95**

Global Spiritual Perspectives

Spiritual Perspectives on America's Role as Superpower

by *the Editors at SkyLight Paths*

Are we the world's good neighbor or a global bully?

Explores broader issues surrounding the use of American power around the world, including in Iraq and the Middle East. From a spiritual perspective, what are America's responsibilities as the only remaining superpower?

Contributors:

Dr. Beatrice Bruteau • Rev. Dr. Joan Brown Campbell • Tony Campolo • Rev. Forrest Church • Lama Surya Das • Matthew Fox • Kabir Helminski • Thich Nhat Hanh • Eboo Patel • Abbot M. Basil Pennington, ocso • Dennis Prager • Rosemary Radford Ruether • Wayne Teasdale • Rev. William McD. Tully • Rabbi Arthur Waskow • John Wilson

5½ x 8½, 256 pp, Quality PB, ISBN 1-893361-81-0 **$16.95**

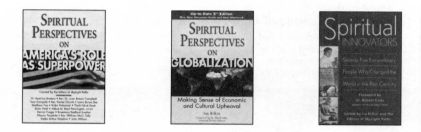

Spiritual Perspectives on Globalization, 2nd Edition
Making Sense of Economic and Cultural Upheaval

by *Ira Rifkin;* Foreword by *Dr. David Little, Harvard Divinity School*

What is globalization? What are spiritually minded people saying and doing about it?

This lucid introduction surveys the religious landscape, explaining in clear and nonjudgmental language the beliefs that motivate spiritual leaders, activists, theologians, academics, and others involved on all sides of the issue. This edition includes a new Afterword and Discussion Guide designed for group use.

5½ x 8½, 256 pp, Quality PB, ISBN 1-59473-045-8 **$16.99**

Spiritual Innovators: *Seventy-Five Extraordinary People Who Changed the World in the Past Century*

Edited by *Ira Rifkin* and *the Editors at SkyLight Paths;* Foreword by *Robert Coles*

Black Elk, Bede Griffiths, H. H. the Dalai Lama, Abraham Joshua Heschel, Martin Luther King, Jr., Krishnamurti, C. S. Lewis, Aimee Semple McPherson, Thomas Merton, Simone Weil, and many more.

Profiles of the most important spiritual leaders of the past one hundred years. An invaluable reference of twentieth-century religion and an inspiring resource for spiritual challenge today. Authoritative list of seventy-five includes mystics and martyrs, intellectuals and charismatics from the East and West. For each, includes a brief biography, inspiring quotes, and resources for more in-depth study.

6 x 9, 304 pp, b/w photographs, Quality PB, ISBN 1-893361-50-0 **$16.95**;
HC, ISBN 1-893361-43-8 **$24.95**

Meditation/Prayer

Finding Grace at the Center: *The Beginning of Centering Prayer*
by *M. Basil Pennington, OCSO, Thomas Keating, OCSO,* and *Thomas E. Clarke, SJ*

The book that helped launch the Centering Prayer "movement." Explains the prayer of *The Cloud of Unknowing,* posture and relaxation, the three simple rules of centering prayer, and how to cultivate centering prayer throughout all aspects of your life.
5 x 7¼, 112 pp, HC, ISBN 1-893361-69-1 **$14.95**

Prayers to an Evolutionary God
by *William Cleary;* Afterword by *Diarmuid O'Murchu*

How is it possible to pray when God is dislocated from heaven, dispersed all around us, and more of a creative force than an all-knowing father? In this unique collection of eighty prose prayers and related commentary, William Cleary considers new ways of thinking about God and the world around us. Inspired by the spiritual and scientific teachings of Diarmuid O'Murchu and Teilhard de Chardin, Cleary reveals that religion and science can be combined to create an expanding view of the universe—an evolutionary faith.
6 x 9, 208 pp, HC, ISBN 1-59473-006-7 **$21.99**

Meditation without Gurus: *A Guide to the Heart of Practice*
by *Clark Strand*

Short, compelling reflections show you how to make meditation a part of your daily life, without the complication of gurus, mantras, retreats, or treks to distant mountains. This enlightening book strips the practice down to its essential heart—simplicity, lightness, and peace—showing you that the most important part of practice is not whether you can get in the full lotus position, but rather your ability to become fully present in the moment.
5½ x 8½, 192 pp, Quality PB, ISBN 1-893361-93-4 **$16.95**

Meditation & Its Practices
A Definitive Guide to Techniques and Traditions of Meditation in Yoga and Vedanta
by *Swami Adiswarananda*

The complete sourcebook for exploring Hinduism's two most time-honored traditions of meditation.

Drawing on both classic and contemporary sources, this comprehensive sourcebook outlines the scientific, psychological, and spiritual elements of Yoga and Vedanta meditation.
6 x 9, 504 pp, HC, ISBN 1-893361-83-7 **$34.95**

Children's Spirituality

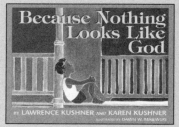

Because Nothing Looks Like God
by *Lawrence and Karen Kushner* Full-color illus. by *Dawn W. Majewski*

For ages 4 & up

MULTICULTURAL, NONDENOMINATIONAL, NONSECTARIAN

Real-life examples of happiness and sadness—from goodnight stories, to the hope and fear felt the first time at bat, to the closing moments of life—introduce children to the possibilities of spiritual life. A vibrant way for children—and their adults—to explore what, where, and how God is in our lives.

11 x 8½, 32 pp, HC, Full-color illus., ISBN 1-58023-092-X **$16.95**

Also available: **Teacher's Guide,** 8½ x 11, 22 pp, PB, ISBN 1-58023-140-3 **$6.95 For ages 5–8**

Where Is God? (A Board Book)

For ages 0–4

by *Lawrence and Karen Kushner;* Full-color illus. by *Dawn W. Majewski*

A gentle way for young children to explore how God is with us every day, in every way. Abridged from *Because Nothing Looks Like God* by Lawrence and Karen Kushner and specially adapted to board book format to delight and inspire young readers.
5 x 5, 24 pp, Board, Full-color illus., ISBN 1-893361-17-9 **$7.95**

What Does God Look Like? (A Board Book)

For ages 0–4

by *Lawrence and Karen Kushner;* Full-color illus. by *Dawn W. Majewski*

A simple way for young children to explore the ways that we "see" God. Abridged from *Because Nothing Looks Like God* by Lawrence and Karen Kushner and specially adapted to board book format to delight and inspire young readers.
5 x 5, 24 pp, Board, Full-color illus., ISBN 1-893361-23-3 **$7.95**

How Does God Make Things Happen? (A Board Book)

For ages 0–4

by *Lawrence and Karen Kushner;* Full-color illus. by *Dawn W. Majewski*

A charming invitation for young children to explore how God makes things happen in our world. Abridged from *Because Nothing Looks Like God* by Lawrence and Karen Kushner and specially adapted to board book format to delight and inspire young readers.
5 x 5, 24 pp, Board, Full-color illus., ISBN 1-893361-24-1 **$7.95**

What Is God's Name? (A Board Book)

For ages 0–4

by *Sandy Eisenberg Sasso;* Full-color illus. by *Phoebe Stone*

Everyone and everything in the world has a name. What is God's name? Abridged from the award-winning *In God's Name* by Sandy Eisenberg Sasso and specially adapted to board book format to delight and inspire young readers.
5 x 5, 24 pp, Board, Full-color illus., ISBN 1-893361-10-1 **$7.99**

Children's Spiritual Biography

Ten Amazing People: *And How They Changed the World*
by *Maura D. Shaw*; Foreword by *Dr. Robert Coles*
Full-color illus. by *Stephen Marchesi*

For ages 7 & up

Black Elk • Dorothy Day • Malcolm X • Mahatma Gandhi • Martin Luther King, Jr. • Mother Teresa • Janusz Korczak • Desmond Tutu • Thich Nhat Hanh • Albert Schweitzer

This vivid, inspirational, and authoritative book will open new possibilities for children by telling the stories of how ten of the past century's greatest leaders changed the world in important ways.
8½ x 11, 48 pp, HC, Full-color illus., ISBN 1-893361-47-0 **$17.95**

A new series:
Spiritual
Biographies
for Young
People

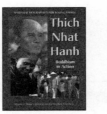   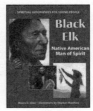

Thich Nhat Hanh: *Buddhism in Action*
by *Maura D. Shaw*; Full-color illus. by *Stephen Marchesi*

For ages 7 & up

Warm illustrations, photos, age-appropriate activities, and Thich Nhat Hanh's own poems introduce a great man to children in a way they can understand and enjoy. Includes a list of important Buddhist words to know.
6¾ x 8¾, 32 pp, HC, Full-color illus., ISBN 1-893361-87-X **$12.95**

Gandhi: *India's Great Soul*
by *Maura D. Shaw*; Full-color illus. by *Stephen Marchesi*

For ages 7 & up

There are a number of biographies of Gandhi written for young readers, but this is the only one that balances a simple text with illustrations, photographs, and activities that encourage children and adults to talk about how to make changes happen without violence. Introduces children to important concepts of freedom, equality, and justice among people of all backgrounds and religions.
6¾ x 8¾, 32 pp, HC, Full-color illus., ISBN 1-893361-91-8 **$12.95**

Dorothy Day: *A Catholic Life of Action*
by *Maura D. Shaw*; Full-color illus. by *Stephen Marchesi*

For ages 7 & up

Introduces children to one of the most inspiring women of the twentieth century, a down-to-earth spiritual leader who saw the presence of God in every person she met. Includes practical activities, a timeline, and a list of important words to know.
6¾ x 8¾, 32 pp, HC, Full-color illus., ISBN 1-59473-011-3 **$12.99**

Black Elk: *Native American Man of Spirit*
by *Maura D. Shaw*; Full-color illus. by *Stephen Marchesi*

For ages 7 & up

Through historically accurate illustrations and photos, inspiring age-appropriate activities, and Black Elk's own words, this colorful biography introduces children to a remarkable person who ensured that the traditions and beliefs of his people would not be forgotten.
6¾ x 8¾, 32 pp, HC, Full-color illus., ISBN 1-59473-043-1 **$12.99**

Religious Etiquette/Reference

How to Be a Perfect Stranger, 3rd Edition: *The Essential Religious Etiquette Handbook*

Edited by *Stuart M. Matlins* and *Arthur J. Magida*

The indispensable guidebook to help the well-meaning guest when visiting other people's religious ceremonies.

A straightforward guide to the rituals and celebrations of the major religions and denominations in the United States and Canada from the perspective of an interested guest of any other faith, based on information obtained from authorities of each religion. Belongs in every living room, library, and office.

COVERS:

African American Methodist Churches • Assemblies of God • Baha'i • Baptist • Buddhist • Christian Church (Disciples of Christ) • Christian Science (Church of Christ, Scientist) • Churches of Christ • Episcopalian and Anglican • Hindu • Islam • Jehovah's Witnesses • Jewish • Lutheran • Mennonite/Amish • Methodist • Mormon (Church of Jesus Christ of Latter-day Saints) • Native American/First Nations • Orthodox Churches • Pentecostal Church of God • Presbyterian • Quaker (Religious Society of Friends) • Reformed Church in America/Canada • Roman Catholic • Seventh-day Adventist • Sikh • Unitarian Universalist • United Church of Canada • United Church of Christ

6 x 9, 432 pp, Quality PB, ISBN 1-893361-67-5 **$19.95**

What You Will See Inside a Mosque

by *Aisha Karen Khan*; Photographs by *Aaron Pepis*

A colorful, fun-to-read introduction that explains the ways and whys of Muslim faith and worship.

Visual and informative, featuring full-page pictures and concise descriptions of what is happening, the objects used, the spiritual leaders and laypeople who have specific roles, and the spiritual intent of the believers.

Ideal for children as well as teachers, parents, librarians, clergy, and lay leaders who want to demystify the celebrations and ceremonies of Islam throughout the year, as well as encourage understanding and tolerance among different faith traditions.

8½ x 10½, 32 pp, Full-color photographs, HC, ISBN 1-893361-60-8 **$16.95**

Or phone, fax, mail or e-mail to: SKYLIGHT PATHS Publishing
Sunset Farm Offices, Route 4 • P.O. Box 237 • Woodstock, Vermont 05091
Tel: (802) 457-4000 • Fax: (802) 457-4004 • www.skylightpaths.com
Credit card orders: (800) 962-4544 (8:30AM–5:30PM ET Monday–Friday)
Generous discounts on quantity orders. SATISFACTION GUARANTEED. Prices subject to change.